EWELL'S MARCH HOME

THE CIVIL WAR AND EARLY TIMES IN AND AROUND GREENWICH, VIRGINIA

EARLE P. BARRON, D. MIN.

Linda Godfrey

Copyright @1999 by Earle P. Barron

ISBN: 0-7392-0219-7

Library of Congress Catalog Card Number: 99-94379

Printed in the USA by

MORRIS PUBLISHING

3212 East Highway 30 • Kearney, NE 68847 • 1-800-650-7888

7/30/99

Love,
Mom & Mamaw

To James L. Cooke
Greenwich historian and friend

PREFACE

This book is about the Civil War and early times in and around Greenwich, Virginia. October 14, 1863, the day of the Battles of Auburn and Bristoe, is the primary time period. General Richard S. Ewell, who grew up two miles from Greenwich on what is now Lonesome Road, is the principal person of interest.

However, the focus of the book is not on the battles that were won or lost. It deals more with the region and some of the people that lived here. I attempt to portray scenes from this particular community as representative of a larger area at this period of time. For the most part, the places and persons were unpretentious and ordinary. But in addition to General Ewell, Charles Green, merchant, and Thomas Balch, Presbyterian pastor and author, stand out as gifted persons.

The first part, "A Long Day - October 14, 1863," takes General Ewell's march from Warrenton to the Battle of Auburn and then up Rogues Road to Greenwich. It then narrates the progress Ewell makes by back roads and fields past his home place, Stoney Lonesome, and finally his arrival at the Battle of Bristoe - all on October 14, 1863. Comments about these places and people are not always restricted to the time period of the Civil War. The second section, "More on Places and People Along the Way," expands some of the accounts of life in this area that are introduced to the reader in the first section.

The Civil War affected life in Prince William and Fauquier Counties considerably and continued to do so for many years. The conflict may have been entered into optimistically in 1861. But early on in Northern Virginia, it is possible to note pessimism and gloom. As death, destruction and destitution increase, so does a sense of despair. This negativism shows up especially in diaries where persons are more honest in expressing their feelings.

But along with this pessimism, there remained hope - hope that if the Confederacy kept fighting long enough, the Union might settle for an equitable peace. Or if not, the personal piety, strong at that time, generated belief that God would intervene for his people.

Despite the hardship and suffering, the War created excitement, and the resulting energy stimulated an otherwise drab existence for many. The challenge brought out unsuspected courage and heroic action as well as petty self-serving in a number of Rebel citizens. Many persons of that period would look back and remember the time as one of grand and glorious days.

It took many years for Northern Virginia to recover from the Civil War. Its destruction scarred the scene for some time, but most of these wounds are now healed. Today, the average citizen has little inkling of the conflict's impact on the territory. In writing this book, I hope to help preserve a few of the stories of people and places which are a part of our history.

I express appreciation to the members and friends of Greenwich Presbyterian Church for encouraging and supporting the writing of this book. In addition, I thank the congregation and several persons who have contributed towards meeting the cost of printing. I am indebted to Linda Godfrey, church secretary, and Colleen Frazier who have been of invaluable service in typing this and other manuscripts in the past. Elaine Yankey has also helped with the typing, and Joanne Canda has been a good proof reader. Don Wilson of the Bull Run Library, Prince William County, has helped me greatly with the correct form for endnotes and bibliography. James Cooke, local historian, has provided much material of historical interest related to the subject. I appreciate the painting for the cover by Dr. Julia Roane, Winchester, Virginia, of the meeting of Generals Ewell, Lee and Hill at Greenwich Presbyterian Church. The original is in the possession of James Cooke.

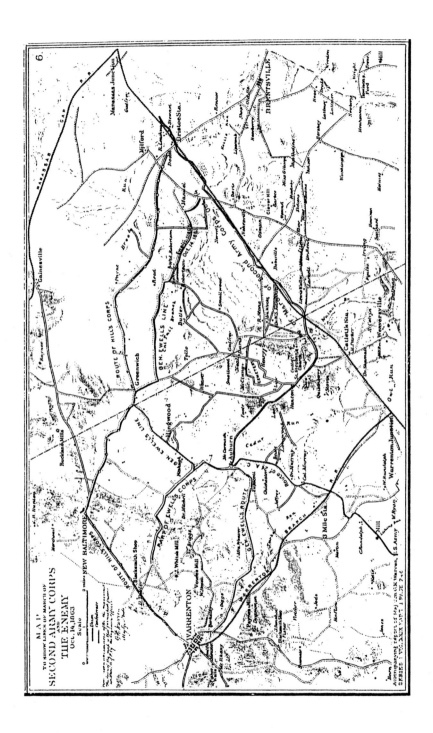

MAP
TO SHOW LINES OF MARCH OF
SECOND ARMY CORPS
AND
THE ENEMY
Oct. 14, 1863

CONTENTS

PART ONE

A LONG DAY - OCTOBER 14, 1863

CHAPTER ONE
A DISTANT DRUM

A Bold Horseman

General Richard S. Ewell, dressed as a Confederate general, wore a straight, short sword in a black, leather scabbard. The silver-hilted rapier had been his grandfather, Jesse Ewell's, in the American Revolution. Dr. Jesse Ewell, Richard's cousin, had given the sword to him when Richard was recuperating from amputation at Dunblane.[1] The General occasionally adjusted the sword to be more comfortable. He sat in the saddle with his left leg stuck out more stiffly than the right. Sometimes, he seemed to grimace as if sharp pains began at a prosthesis on the end of the stump and ran up to his thigh.

Most of the time Ewell appeared to ignore the discomfort. He had lost his leg at the Second Battle of Manassas not far from where he was headed. (It was his second injury of the War. He had been the first Confederate officer hit by enemy fire near Fairfax, Virginia). Later at Gettysburg, in a fusillade of bullets, Brigadier John B. Gordon heard an ominous thud. He asked the General if he were all right. He replied that he wasn't hurt. It didn't hurt to be wounded in a wooden leg.[2]

Ewell weighed a little over 140 pounds and was fairly tall for his day. In 1865 he wrote his sister, Rebecca, that his height was at 5 feet 10 1/2 inches assuming that both legs were present. But they weren't, and actual height was then about 5 feet 8 inches.[3] He sported a beard, but on his crown he had no hair. He had large ears and nose with lots of wrinkles on his face. His most striking feature was penetrating eyes. At 46 he showed signs of aging as well as chronic poor health, though he had a military manner that said, "I am an officer."

Ewell was practical minded and intelligent, sometimes cynical and sharp-tongued. He had lots of nervous energy and a bad temper. After he married his cousin, Lizinka Brown, he became less irascible. He liked alcohol but hated tobacco smoke and being around it.

Many of his troops and fellow officers admired him, but General Robert E. Lee may have had some doubts about Ewell's ability as a commander. Some thought that Ewell had not really wanted the job as leader of the Second Corps. They believed he had liked being under General Thomas J. Jackson when he was alive and felt that he had served better in that capacity.

Ewell knew that Lee liked the offensive; so did he. At First Manassas he let it be known that he wanted to pursue the Yankees after their defeat. Following Gettysburg, when Lee made the strategic move to take the pressure off of Northern Virginia and get into Union territory again, he did not object. If Lee could cut off a portion of General George G. Meade's army, the Confederates believed they would win a victory that way. To do so on October 14, 1863 it would be necessary to intercept Meade before he crossed Broad Run. This might force a battle to the South's advantage.[4]

On October 14, 1863, Ewell was riding through the part of the country where he had grown up and which he loved. Here he had spent as much time as possible outdoors. He had done almost everything a boy would like to do - fishing, hunting and often racing horses about the hollows and high places of Prince William and Fauquier Counties. He had developed considerable skill as a rider which came in handy the rest of his life, particularly in the army out West. In the Civil War, he was a "bold horseman."

October 13, the day before, Ewell and his Second Corps had left Fauquier White Sulfur Springs at dawn and gotten into Warrenton between 10:00 AM and 2:00 PM. While waiting, the General visited friends, and he accepted an invitation to an evening meal with a distant relative.

4

Troops Marching

The locals were glad to see Confederate troops. But they were upset with the Union forces marching backwards and forwards across their land. Elizabeth Frances Gray, who lived between Warrenton and Auburn near the branches of Cedar Run, took up her pen and wrote in her diary on October 13, 1863. "A drum is distantly heard in Warrenton. The servant reports the Yanks upon us again."[5] She saw a group moving up towards the house and braced to meet them. Later, however, she said she was glad to discover that they were Rebels. She noted that the Army was passing the Double Poplars, and she reported that she heard heavy booming of canon that evening over by Auburn. She thrilled at the sight of bright lights from brilliant campfires and rejoiced to hear the howls and hurrahs of Southern voices, a sound she had been missing for some time. She could even pick up distant strains of "Bonny Blue Flag" from the band in Warrenton, or at least she thought she could.

Braying Mules

Lee sent General "Jeb" Stuart to keep tabs on the Army of the Potomac as it retreated towards Washington along the Orange and Alexandria Railroad. In the process, Stuart found himself caught in the woods, undetected, between Union Major General William H. French's Third Corps and Major General Governear K. Warren's Second Corps. Stuart lay low between Auburn and St. Stephen's Episcopal Church all night but was afraid his hungry, braying mules would give away his presence. Lee, learning of Stuart's plight, sent General Ewell and his Second Corps to rescue the cavalry unit.

Stuart hid close to Elmwood, the home of William Edmond Fitzhugh. William may have at one time had a school on his place. When Ewell's mother Elizabeth decided that she had taught Richard all the reading, writing and arithmetic she could at home, utilizing his father's large library, she decided to get him to a professional. In 1834 she found enough money to send him to study at a Fitzhugh home in Fauquier County.[6] Ewell had only one year there, but during that time he underwent the study of classics under The Rev. Mr. Knox who was renown locally. He did attend further classes at Greenville, which may have been the old Ewell place near Stoney Lonesome, with his brother Tom. He may not have mastered all subjects but, at least he was a good enough student to get in West Point. His brother Ben, who later became president of William & Mary, had attended the Academy before him.[7]

A High Hill

October 13, the day before Ewell had begun his March, the air had been cool but brilliantly clear. Fall foliage had taken on many colors and hues. However, on the morning of October 14 at 5 AM, when Ewell left Warrenton, a thick fog rolled over all the low places. It was difficult to make out much of the route as the units headed south on Dumfries Road. Ewell crossed Baldwin Ridge in the darkness, home territory to diary writer Gray. She lived at Millview off of Dumfries Road about half of a mile east of the present State Route 674 in the area of the Terranova Subdivision. Later Elizabeth Francis Gray married Warren Fitzhugh.[8]

Ewell passed by Baldwin Ridge Episcopal Church at the intersection of Dumfries and Baldwin Ridge Road. At one time, Baldwin Ridge Road, a trail of sorts, went all the way to Double Poplars Road and came out at Double Poplars Church. Other portions of Ewell's Second Corps had taken the Double Poplars Road to Auburn from Warrenton.

A Thick Fog

At around 6:15 AM, dawn revealed a cloudy day with patches of fog to troops near Auburn. Auburn was a small village at first called Barnett's Tavern. George Neavil's Mill, originally built in 1712, had ground grain and was still running there. The mill was purchased by William Fitzhugh in 1811 and the estate of Warren Fitzhugh sold it to John Grant in 1884.[9] Also Neavil had operated a tavern which had been discontinued. George Washington had lodged there in 1748.[10]

On the hillside to the northwest, stood the homeplace and shop of Stephen McCormick, inventor in 1816 of a cast-iron plow which greatly facilitated farming. The farm implement plowed deeper and required fewer horses to pull than earlier plows.

Stephen's father gave his young son a horse but was upset when he caught Stephen racing. He ordered him to hitch his steed to the plow and go to work. Stephen, disgusted with the old wooden plow that didn't perform well, later invented his own.[11] By the 1840's, the manufacturer in Auburn had 12 models and had sold 10,000 plows in Virginia and other Southern states.[12]

Ewell had gotten an early interest in agriculture, learning not only how to raise horses but also to farm. It may be assumed that he had heard a great deal about Stephen and also his brother, Cyrus, who had invented the reaper and greatly appreciated these labor saving advances.

Other than a few houses, not much stood in Auburn on the morning of October 14. At any rate, soldiers on both sides couldn't see a whole lot because of the thick fog which filled the cut of Cedar Run through the town. Visibility seemed somewhat better on the steep hillsides above the villages. At sunrise Ewell attacked. There was considerable cannonading that both Union and Southern forces could hear miles away. Locals were roused by the same thunder. Diarist Gray wrote that she was shaken out of sleep by the booming of canon on October 14, 1863, a roar that lasted all day. Fighting took place just two miles from her home. She thought the Rebels were winning, but she wasn't sure. But the apparent victory made the day a spicy one, the best since the war began. She was startled by nearby bursting shells and deafened by the roar of muskets. It seemed to her that soldiers were running around in all directions, and apparently she helped feed some breakfast. She noted that Fitzhugh Lee's division came close to her grandmother's place. After all the cannonading, she and the family walked on Baldwin Ridge. Smoke from the artillery still hung in the valleys.

Though not decisive, the engagement freed Stuart who joined in the battle. But the fighting also delayed the Confederates in catching up with the main body of Union General Meade's forces by at least four hours.

CHAPTER TWO
ROGUES ROAD

At the end of the battle of Auburn, U.S. General Warren retreated to Catlett's Station and Lee directed Ewell to Greenwich to meet up with General A. P. Hill. With the sun higher in the sky and the fog lifted, General Ewell could make out the countryside which he knew so well. As the Corps moved along the Old Carolina or Rogues Road towards Greenwich, he noticed familiar landmarks. He must have been saddened to see the state of the fields, missing fences and burned buildings. He could easily observe that life had been hard on the people and places in the area.

Trying Times

Even under so called normal conditions, a number of poor whites had little to eat. As the war progressed, some of the yeoman farmers and more affluent landowners lived without enough food to prevent serious nutritional deficiencies. Some had pellagra. (On occasion, concoctions of flour, straw and saw dust with a little grease and sometime molasses were fed to the Confederate troops.[1]) The farms were generally poor because the shallow topsoil had been exhausted. Locals had about quit trying to raise crops and animals because troops of one side or the other were sure to take them.

The year had started badly according to *The Diary of Courthouse Square*.

> 1863 - Now came a terrible winter. The Yankees occupying Warrenton needed wood to burn and since the crosses in the cemetery were convenient, they were used for firewood. That left all those graves nameless. The train engines burned coal as long as they had it, but when that ran out

anything along the tracks made of wood was used. April 5th, Easter Sunday, had 9 to 10 inches of snow with a temperature of 31 degrees... But there were no buds on the trees and no planting had been done. It was the "dreariest, coldest, wettest, saddest winter followed by the latest spring within the memory of man," someone said. Even on May 1st, people still wore winter clothes, gardens were not cleaned, trees still did not have many leaves and, of course, the corn wasn't in nor much grass to be ready for hay.(51) Some wondered if it were a punishment for their actions. Was the Almighty unhappy with the country?[2]

Perhaps Ewell didn't wonder about God's opinion, but likely he was unhappy with the horrible condition of the area.

Great Depredation

Jacksie Howison, also discontent, wrote in her diary of foragers.[3]

April 19, 1862. The Yankeys have been committing great depredations in that and the upper neighborhoods, have been to Mr. Carnall, took about $350 worth from him in way of grain, meat, potatoes, tallow & various other things; Mr. C.'s Gold Watch & good many other things about the house that they could very easily done without. Killed one of Miss Lizzie's turkeys right before us all & would have killed more if she had not begged him so hard not to kill them. There was about 100 men & 25 naggers, there has been a good many here also, but I rejoice to hear they acted like gentlemen ought to act. I am glad to hear there are some honorable men in the Northern Army.

May 2, 1862. Ah! no one knows but me, and my God, what I have undergone in the last 6 months, and now my first trouble is as great as it was six months ago. But I must not complain, the son of Man once had not where to lay his head."

August 3, 1863. Again with my pen in hand I am seated to write in my journal. There has been plenty of those disgusting monsters here today. I think there is only one thing worse that they could have done that they did not do. They took my journal too this and one other sheet is all they left. Isn't it too bad, I would rather they had taken the nicest dress or almost anything I have. I have been keeping a journal ever since I was fifteen and all the most important things of my life were written down. I was afraid they would take it and I put it upstairs in a counterpane folded up, but the rogues found it.

On October 9, 1862 Gray wrote that nothing seemed worse than being surrounded by a "lawless army" that they didn't know. She felt that they would be lucky not to be robbed of all possessions. Mt. Airy had been ransacked and left destitute of every comfort. Every bit of goods and provisions that had been laid in was gone. Soldiers had searched every nook and corner and turned her once rich grandmother of 80 years or more into a poverty-stricken old lady. For Gray, this was too sad to even think about. She could only pray that the foragers would met with their just reward.

Jackson later noted some good news.

November 22, 1863. Oh! I like to forgot to say I have found my journal. I thought the Yankeys had taken. I accused them of stealing wrongfully for since I had put it away and did not remember

where it was. That is frequently the case, we hide
things from the Yankeys and then can't find them
ourselves. Miss Lizzie says she knows she can't
find all the things she has put away.

My Poor Bereaved Parents

The local people experienced not only privation and various
indignities but also grief. Gray related the shock of hearing about
the death of her brother January 29, 1862. Sometime later the
family discovered he had been wounded and was a prisoner in
Nashville. Eventually he was exchanged and returned home. But
later, December 27, 1862, she wrote the family had received word
that brother F was wounded in fighting at Fredericksburg.
Corpsmen took him to Richmond. F's father found him, but he
died very soon afterwards. Gray expressed considerable pain for
herself. She also said, "Lord, be with my poor bereaved parents &
help them to bear thy chasting rod & sanctify all things to thy
good." She went on to recount the 17 months of hard soldiering
he had borne; she declared how much a hero he had been as he
fought many hard battles. She said that all that knew him would
suffer his loss. She wondered if the Lord had been the one who had
taken him away.

It Seems So Hard

Locals also suffered as a result of brushes between
Northern and Southern outfits. On May 14, 1863, a Federal party
came upon a group of Confederates at the Marsteller place near
Warrenton Junction. At least three were wounded on each side,
and homeowner Marsteller was killed. In her diary Jacksie says

May 17, 1863. Nothing but distress and
trouble in this section of country it seems, since the
Yankees have been here. Last Thursday morning a
company went to Mr. Marstella's and there was

12

four gentlemen there, 2 South Caroleans and 2 of Mr. M's. sons, they killed 2 and wounded 3 or 4 of the Yankees, but worse than all they killed poor Oceola, and he not a soldier. Don't it seem too bad he was afraid they would take him prisoner as they have taken so many men (citizens) and he hid in the garden but they saw him and shot him, supposed he was a soldier I reckon. Poor girls I do feel so much for them. They have, I believe, four brothers in the Army and it does seem so hard that the only one at home should be killed.

William A. Brent lived at Brenton, near Marshall. He and three brothers fought in the War. One was killed, and he and the others were wounded several times. Billy rode with John S. Mosby and was a member of Company A, Seventh Virginia Cavalry. He wrote of the Marsteller incident and located it at the home of Mr. Arrell Marsteller which may have been "Arrelton." It once stood on the location of the north side of the present Fitzwater Drive, halfway between Manley and Burwell Roads. He said

The Marsteller boys were all good fighters. On one occasion two of them, Yucatan and Alpfar, with two other soldiers, were surprised in their father's house before day by a party of Federals... They were in bed when they heard the sound of horses' feet, and only had time to put on their clothes when they heard the Federals coming upstairs. They met them, drove them back and into the parlor, and out into the yard, where two were killed, and though the house was surrounded by a Company and there was a Regiment waiting in sight, they opened their way, got to their horses which had been kept tied, bridled and saddled, in a secret place, and rode away. The parlor and

13

stairway were filled with bullet holes. Yucatan Marsteller was quite lame in the right leg, which had been paralyzed by a shot on top of the head, which tore the skull away to the brain.

But when they had gone, their old father and sisters had to pay terribly for this. Another son, who was not a soldier. . .was killed near the house in a piece of pines as he was returning home; and a servant woman, a little brother and his sisters, had to load his remains in a horsecart and bring them to the house.[4]

Reading, Writing - and Soldiers

Despite such trails, Northern Virginians tried to keep up the quality of their lives. This included getting an education. Near the intersection of the present Rogues and Ringwood Road, Ewell passed Ringwood on his right. Ringwood Manse, formerly the home of Rev. Thomas Balch, was at this time Ringwood Academy, a school for girls. At Balch's encouragement, and with Balch's support, Jane Alexander Milligan founded and ran the seminary which accommodated about 14 girls.

Balch was a published writer with a perky style and lots of allusions to the classics penned. He wrote,

Would that we could say the same of Ringwood, my once happy home, which stands about five miles from my present abode. The war did it no good, but the injury will soon be repaired. Hope so, for that spot is associated with thirteen years of my hermit life.[5]

Jacksie wrote in January 31, 1864 that she was very much interested in Ringwood Academy and that she was anxious to go to school there the coming spring and summer. But she was concerned that it was a "good smart walk" for her alone, and she was afraid to go by herself in the perilous times. She enrolled on May 9, 1864 and wrote that she had been busy studying all evening, to the point of dozing off. She listed her subjects as "Reading, Writing, Arithmetic, Geography, Gramma, Philosophy & Astronomy besides Exercise in Composition & Scholars Companion." Not only did the girls study such basics, but every morning they had to say a Scripture lesson which consisted of repeating a certain number of verses from the Bible.

But there were times for other activities - especially soldiers. One day she visited with one at school, and when she got home there were three more to see her. But even though she was busy studying and socializing she sometimes got down in the dumps. On November 30, 1864 she wrote,

> I have just returned from Ringwood. Miss Janie had an examination this morn, quite a nice little time. Some of the girls performed splendidly. It seems that I often feel sad. I don't know why I am sad today, nothing has been said to wound my feelings as is sometimes the case, yet I am sad. Oh! that I had someone to whom I could go, to tell all my trials and difficulties, one that could sympathize with me and feel for me, as I am sure none on earth does or can. But O may these thoughts make me close, close to Him who hast promised at all times to be near, to comfort & cheer the lonely. O God, be to me a friend.

Diarist Gray attended Ringwood also and apparently boarded there. She developed an infatuation with Aunt Belle, Janie Milligan's sister, that she remembered as amusing in later years. She may have studied some but enjoyed being "mothered" and the social opportunities more.

On September 20, 1861 she wrote that she had gotten to know many nice gentlemen soldiers from the Deep South. Many of them stayed close to Ringwood and visited daily. This made Ringwood a sweet spot for all the girls there in the summer of 1861. She also enjoyed being near her dear Aunt Belle, Janie Milligan's sister, who had married a Fitzhugh. Aunt Belle always made gloomy days bright for her. "She was easy for all to love," Gray said.

By October 10, the pleasant company had been disrupted as soldier friends had to go back to camp. The young ladies at Ringwood descended into gloom. But the darkness vanished when two soldiers surprised her about noon. They stayed for a meal. But it now seemed "cold & stiff" to Gray. A dark cloud had come over the happy place and some of those present.

As the war went on, she often felt sad. She said on December 22, 1862 that the postal service had brought bad news of her brother French who had been seriously wounded in the back. Doctors said he wouldn't live, and he lay paralyzed in Richmond. Gray's father started for Culpeper to try to get to Richmond. The thought of French not living was too unhappy a thought for Gray to consider.

Then again on December 25 she wrote that the past Christmas at Ringwood had been a happy time with young folks feeling bright and cheerful. But the sad affect of the war had dashed bright hopes of any kind of peace. She could only sigh about the failure of peace and the end of war and pray.

She and others attended prayer meetings at Ringwood. Apparently the teachers and the girls were very religious. Miss Milligan required all the girls to go to church at Greenwich Presbyterian Church.[6] They often went to services in an ox cart. Uncle Jim French, perhaps a servant, drove the cart. Usually they made it a day's outing, combining visitation with worship. It was not uncommon for them to take their dinner in case of a "long sermon & slow horse," Gray said on October 25, 1862. Sometimes she enjoyed the sermon, but most always she liked the social activities on the pleasant day's excursions. On the way and back, they talked of many things, apparently even the preaching. On October 4, 1862, she wrote that Mr. Balch had an excellent sermon. Aunt Kate Nickens who lived on the place at that time, a free black, said the girls would go singing.[7]

The Power of the Sword

Passing by Ringwood, Ewell moved up the road towards Greenwich. The General came to the home of George Warren Fitzhugh who lived at Grapewood. Later Fitzhugh married diary writer Gray. He was an elder at Greenwich Church and is buried there. He was also a member of the Black Horse Cavalry, as were other members of the family, William Dedman and perhaps Thomas Fitzhugh. This fighting outfit began with a gathering of Warrenton lawyers. It led a successful charge against the Union Army at the First Battle of Manassas. The unit seemed to have operated in such a fashion as to sometimes be considered a guerrilla troop by Union soldiers.

At Grapewood, Ewell looked up at the farmhouse. There had been a skirmish in the lane nearby between some of John S. Mosby's men and troopers form the Fifth New York Cavalry just that spring. Mosby and his men attacked a train on the Orange & Alexandria Railroad near Catlett's Station on May 30, 1863. Mosby had with him what he called a mountain howitzer which made him less mobile. It changed his escape tactics somewhat, so he wasn't able to disperse in all directions as usual. With the Federals in pursuit, some of his men headed through Greenwich past Charles Green's house, dropping what was once fresh shad and leather from the railroad raid as they went. Mosby, taking another route, stopped and fired the howitzer a couple of times to his advantage as the Union soldiers in pursuit charged in columns of four. Eventually Mosby reached what is now called Mosby's Lane, just at the south entrance to the present Vint Hill Farms Station on Rogues Road. Mosby waited at a bend in the road and stopped his pursuers with pistol fire at close range, his favorite tactics. In the confusion he generated, he charged.

At Mosby's side was Captain Bradford S. Hoskins, small but muscular, a soldier of fortune who was expert with the sword.

An Englishman, he was the son of an Anglican clergyman. He had served of late in her Majesty's Forty-Fourth Regiment of Foot. He had been in the Crimean War, had become tired of garrison life, sold his commission and fought with the Italian patriot Garibaldi in his Sicilian campaign. Hoskins wanted action, and with Mosby he found it.

Mosby said that Hoskins acted in the tradition of the ancient knights. The power of the sword still drove him. The Captain was in the very act of a saber thrust when a Yankee shot him. He fell mortally wounded.

Mosby managed to escape, and his party scattered, but he lost the howitzer. Several men on both sides were killed, and a number more of Mosby's men were captured.

Charles Green and Elias Brooks, his black servant, appeared on the scene of carnage. Green, also an Englishman, went among the wounded offering aid. One he helped was Yankee Lieutenant Barker, hit in the leg in the initial charge. Barker remembered that Green gave him ice water and brandy and invited him to remain at his house until he got well. But Barker declined. Green did take Hoskins and Lieutenant Samuel F. Chapman to his home. One of Green's sons, Douglas, had to give up his bed to the wounded. Chapman recovered, but Hoskins died.[8]

Green notified Hoskin's father, an Anglican clergyman, who sent over money for a monument. The unattractive marker in the Greenwich Presbyterian Cemetary is topped by a concrete cross which bears the inscription "In Hoc Signo Vincos" (In This Sign You Will Conquer) suggesting that the cross is more powerful than the sword. It is not uncommon for Mosby enthusiasts to visit what has become to them a sacred site. Often small Confederate flags are found on the grave. Hoskins seems to draw increasing attraction and interest.

James Cooke said that Ned Taylor was up early that fearful day too.[9] He had been relieved of duty in the Confederate Army after the Battle of Seven Pines. He stayed at home with a minieball in his knee. He showed up shortly after the skirmish at Mosby's lane. He later told of the incident to his grandson, Oakley Taylor, who recounted the story to James Cooke. Taylor struck his heel on the ground and quoted, "Son, the wheels of the cannon sat right here, and the dead horses were so thick in the lane you could not walk up it." Oakley lived in the house now located next door to Oakdale Baptist Church, in Green on Rogues Road. He was a veteran of World War I.

Dollars From Heaven

Just north of Mosby's Lane lay Vint Hill. The name Vint Hill dates back to 1772 when vineyards covered the knolls. During the Civil War, it belonged to Andrew Low. Andrew, born in Liverpool, England in 1839, sailed to Canada on the clipper ship, "Dreadnought." He lived for a time with his parents in Gault but moved to Greenwich when his uncle Charles Green, asked him to oversee his farm at Greenwich. He stayed only a short time before he returned for two years to England to complete his education.

On July 20, 1859 he came back to Virginia. At the age of 20, he was tall, slender with brown hair and blue eyes. That same year he married Elizabeth Scott Moxley. During the same summer, he took Charles Green's advice and purchased Vint Hill, a farm of 1,027 acres. As soon as the transaction was complete the seller told him, "I will give you three years to starve on it." Andrew Low was a hard worker, however, and soon had the place in good order. He remained a British subject all his life and did not participate in the Civil War, though he had a brother, Josiah Low, who fought with the Rebels. Union forces provided a guard for his farm's protection, and the family suffered no deprivation during its course. Graves on the property, unmarked, from the War period are soldiers of the time.

During the War his wife sat with a baby in her lap before the fireplace. A summer storm blew up, and wind and rain came down the chimney. Some of the chimney stones loosened, and to her amazement she saw two or three gold pieces roll across the hearth. Still more gold pieces fell all over the floor, and she had great fun picking them up. Andrew, soon coming in, explained how he had kept his money in gold because of the war and had hidden it in the chimney as the safest place for its protection.[9]

Low raised sheep, cattle and horses and did well, but in 1910 after the death of his wife he moved to Haymarket. He and members of his family are buried at Greenwich. The farm passed through different owners, and during World War II it became Vint Hill Farms Military Stations which has recently been closed. The home still stands.

Don't Shoot

One night at Vint Hill, William A. Brent managed to slip by the Yankees. On October 5, 1863, Billy, who was detached from his unit as a scout, went with a party to disrupt the railroad near Catlett. He and his small group ran into a Federal patrol. During the skirmish, Brent grabbed a Union horse by the bar of its cavalry bit. The rider shot him under the right nipple. He in return fired, and the rider of the horse cried, "I am killed, don't shoot." Brent pulled the trigger again, and the soldier fell off his horse dead.

Brent's compatriots took the wounded Brent to the home of Mr. Arrell Marsteller, "an old gentleman who knew no fear of consequences..." Marsteller's nephew, Dr. Tascoe [Tasker?] Mitchell, whom Brent knew, was there and tended to him. On the 14th of October, he observed Federal troops around Marsteller's home. After the 15th when Lee retired south, he watched foragers in the yard through a window in his room on the first floor. The guard posted by Union officers to keep down foraging didn't know he was there.

After some of Mosby's men captured a Federal officer there, Brent was afraid to remain on the premises. His father came to get him. Those attending to him bandaged him tightly with a broad strip of cotton and put his father's long black circular cloak over his shoulders to conceal his uniform. They rode toward home. Near Greenwich he ran into a cavalry camp. The party flanked it and approached Andrew Low's barn. A Yankee soldier came out and asked them some questions but didn't detain them.

They proceeded to a Dr. Moss's who gave him a stiff toddy, breakfast and rest. He ended up at Dr. Silas B. Hunton's for the night, and his father returned for him the next day and took him to Brenton, his home. He survived the war but was wounded again. He never married and died at Brenton, on October 4, 1904.[11]

Good Yankees

Just beyond Vint Hill, but not quite to Greenwich, the road runs along a fairly high ridge. General Ewell got a good view of the Bull Run Mountain chain from that position. He had actually crossed the tail end of the range when he came down the Dumfries Road at its high point near Baldwin Ridge.

In looking toward the mountain, he turned in the direction of the Blackwell house, off the now Vint Hill Road, close to Lake Manassas. The Blackwell house probably dated back into the 1700's.[12] Two chimneys graced each end. It took a lot of wood to keep the fireplace burning. Ripley Robinson, whose mother has lived there, said one day that Anne Blackwell was sent to get wood for the fire, but she was gone so long her parents went to find her. She was sitting on a big gatepost behind the slave quarters. A large sheep had chased her up a big gate post. She said, "I'm waiting for him to go to roost so I can get down."

During the war, it was the residence of William Blackwell, Ripley's great grandfather. William Spark Blackwell served in Company A, Fourth Virginia Cavalry (Prince William). He later taught school at Greenwich. He is buried at Greenwich Church cemetery. Nannie Blackwell who lived there, married Dr. Robert White, later a minister at Greenwich. In his old age, he developed mental trouble, fell out of the upstairs window and broke his neck in the flowerbed. He and Nannie are buried at Greenwich.

Another great grandfather of Ripley's also had connections with the house. Henry Hancock Lee, V, was born near Lee's Mill on the Rappahanock River. He was with Company H, Fourth

Virginia Cavalry (Black Horse). Henry's wife and son, Harry Lee, lived there at the Blackwell house in Greenwich during the war. Union soldiers came in looking for valuables, cut open a feather bed and poured syrup and preserves on the feathers. The little boy crawled around on the floor and licked the feathers which stuck to him. He said, "Aren't these good Yankees to bring us the sweets."

There was a small room under the flight to the attic and part of the upstairs called the "Apple Room." In the stairway, it was possible to remove a riser. One day Henry Hancock Lee and William Blackwell slipped between the treads to hide from the Yankees. The ladies slid the riser back, and although the Federals searched thoroughly they could not find them. Lee had a cold at the time and had trouble keeping from coughing because he had stirred up so much dust. The house later burned, the fire so hot "you could [read] the Warrenton paper by the light a mile away," said Ripley.

Norfolk Blues

As Ewell looked ahead he could see a lot of dust and heard a lot of noise, the sight and sound of marching troops and creaking wagons other than his own. John Walters of the Norfolk Blues, an artillery unit, had made the trip toward Bristoe another way, through New Baltimore and down the now Vint Hill Road. The day before, he had to wait for the passing of Ewell's wagon train at Hazel River. In his diary he commented on the desolation and destruction he saw and the land overrun with weeds and pine brush as he approached Warrenton. Chimneys stood lonely and gaunt.

On October 14 near New Baltimore, he stopped for a moment to answer a question put to him by one of the ladies along the road. Six battalions of about 100 guns interrupted his romancing. He quickly followed. They went "through the sweet little village of Greenwich, all around which last night's campfires of the Yankees are still burning. On still, over roads and through fields, catching every now and then the sound of Ewell's cannon far off in our right."[13] He didn't get to Bristoe in time for the battle.

When Ewell realized the traffic jam ahead, he was afraid he wouldn't get there at a good time either. A number of plans must have gone through his mind as he turned towards the center of the village. He decided on a detour.

CHAPTER THREE
HAMLET ON A HILL

Balch described the small community just ahead of Ewell.

> The village or rather the hamlet of Greenwich stands more than two miles from the Manse. Tis on a hill, and commands a fine view of the Bull Run. On the southern edge of Greenwich stands another kiosk, reared by another Savannah gentleman; whose name is Sorrel, a native of one of the Carribean islands, perhaps Martinique. At the Northwest of the settlement is a cottage which was occupied by an English lady from Liverpool, England. Her cottage was called "Leasowes". . . Upon the breaking out of the war she went to Canada, and her home was occupied by a gentleman whose name was Jourdan. Jourdan was taken prisoner by McCabe and sent to several prisons. He reached home, but soon after, died. Sorrel's Kiosk was burnt.[1]

Why Did You Burn My Pretty House?

One of the first places Ewell observed at the outskirts of the village of Greenwich was that of his cousins, the Sorrels, near the corner of the present Greenwich and Vint Hill Roads. James Cooke, local historian, says that sometime during the war the elder Sorrel was visiting Charles Greene in Green's Savannah residence. When Green offered his home to Union General Sherman for his headquarters, Sorrel could not hold back anger at the loss of his home and blurted out, "Why did you burn down my pretty house in Greenwich?"

His son, Gilbert Moxley Sorrel, was in Savannah at the outbreak of the war working in a bank. He caught a train right away to Manassas, went to his father's place, borrowed a horse to get to the troops, enlisted and was in the first battle of Manassas. Ewell knew him well. At Malvern Hill, Ewell's unit suffered heavy losses. The exhausted general grabbed a nap on the floor of a shanty near the front. When the door opened, he jerked awake. Ewell who lisped, recognizing Captain G. Moxley Sorrel, challenged him. He wanted to know, "'Mather Sorrel, can you tell me why we had five hundred men killed dead on this field yesterday?'"[2]

Diagonally across from that corner, in front of the Greenwich Presbyterian Church and behind the present house there now, stood the James K. Moore residence. At the time of writing, Mrs. Mae Ellis, a descendant of the Moores and owner of the house, is 107 years of age and the oldest living member of Greenwich Presbyterian Church. Mae Ellis said Greenwich Presbyterian's old log church was on the corner of Vint Hill and Greenwich Roads in front of her house. The old well there was dug by Daniel House, an ancestor of hers. Just across Greenwich Road, on the corner, Daniel House had a store. Will Dulen had another store where Mayhugh's store is now located.[3]

An Ordinary

A little further east, at the intersection of the present Vint Hill and Burwell Roads stood Thornton's Tavern or Ordinary. It had been built as early as 1759 and remains until demolished in 1972. The word, ordinary, sometimes used for taverns in early days, meant the place where a proprietor served a meal regularly at the same price. Taverns were often rough but they dispensed food, liquor and had a fire to ward off the cold. Ordinaries also acted as neighborhood social centers and contact points for other places and people.

For instance, when President elect Thomas Jefferson, traveling from Monticello, made his way for his inauguration in

Washington, D. C., he came close to Greenwich. He bought fodder at Elk Run in Fauquier County, passed by Slate Run Church and then came to the intersection of Brentsville Road (State Route 649) and Dumfries Road (State Route 234) on the edge of what is now Manassas. He ate his evening meal and spent the night at Brown's Tavern or ordinary. In his diary, Jefferson described Brown's Tavern as "a poor house, but obliging people."

At the time Ewell entered Greenwich, the tavern building belonged to Charles Green and was used by caretakers, visitors or members of his family for a residence.

She Turned Her Back

Diagonally across the street from the ordinary stood another old house also owned by Green. It likewise was used by members of Green's family and his many guests. It later became known as the Veeder Place.

Mrs. Veeder, who was Charles Green's daughter, inherited the Veeder properties as her portion of Charles Green's estate. She felt she had been slighted. She never sat down unless she turned the back of her chair toward the Lawn, said James Cooke. Mrs. Mae Ellis, says that Ringwood Seminary met at the house for a time. Her mother attended Ringwood. The building, in good repair, still stands close to the road. Green purchased the property from John Kulp in 1856. Kulp also sold land and his blacksmith shop to James K. Moore about the same time. Kulp may have operated the nearby store.

In 1861 Confederate General P.G.T. Beauregard led a portion of his troops into the first Battle of Manassas through the village of Greenwich. The forces turned off U.S. Route 29 onto State Route 215 and likely camped around Greenwich. Tradition says that Beauregard was entertained at the Veeder Place or the Green House.[4]

Charles Green's house, The Lawn, stood south across the road from the Veeder Place. Balch described it as a "Swiss cottage. . . shaped like the house of Helvetia."[5] Charles Green was born in Shropshire, England, 1807. He came to America and became a prosperous merchant in Savannah, Georgia. Green had a sister in the Greenwich community whom he visited. He also established a sheepfarm near the church. Some relate the name Greenwich to Greenwich, England. Others insist that it is related to the Green family. "Wick" or "Wych" is a suffix meaning "a salt lick," and some believe that Mr. Green's farm adjacent to the church property had such a valuable asset. Nearby settlers referred to this spot near the Old Carolina Road as the one near the "Greenwick."

Green eventually met and took as his second wife Mrs. Aminta Moxley's grand-daughter, Lucy Ireland (1828 - 1867). In 1850 he added to The Lawn 22 1/2 acres which he purchased for $3,000 from Mrs. A.E. Moxley. He later bought more acres for the place.

Union soldier, John C. Gray, Jr., bivouaced nearby, wrote a letter to his mother, August 2, 1863. He said he was impressed with Green's house and property which was located across from the church on the corner of what is now Vint Hill (State Route 215) and Burwell (State Route 604) Roads. He said that the Head Quarters, lst Division, 11th Corps was camped on the lawn of the Englishman. Green had posted on his gate, "British Property under Safeguard, by order of General Mead."[6] He provided meals and lodging for the general, which may have aroused some consternation with local, loyal Southerners. Gray told his mother that he was surprised to find such a clean house in Virginia!

Charles Green, though a cotton merchant in Savannah and a farmer in Greenwich, maintained his British citizenship. He flew an English flag over The Lawn as he called it. During the war, it was also used as a Confederate hospital.[7]

In between Union Generals, Charles Green also entertained Confederate Colonel John S. Mosby and his men. These raiders continually harassed the enemy in this area by capturing supplies and fighting skirmishes. Granddaughter, Ann Green, said that one afternoon Edward, Green's son, crept unnoticed into the parlor to watch Mosby lay "his pumped felt on the piano and is trilling and banging away at the instrument as he roars a thunderous song." Edward crawled behind the hero and fingered his braided coat and examined a coat tail and murmured "Poor fella, poor fella."[8] The breeches were torn and full of patches. Mosby managed to keep poverty out of sight by sitting on it, said Anne Green. Anne, Edward's daughter, also noted that a photograph of Edward from this time showed him to be afflicted with the same problem. Times were tough.

Ann's brother, author Julian Green, just recently died in his nineties. He was a member of the prestigious Academy Francaise. They had to make him an honorary Frenchman to do so. Julian did most of his writing in French, but wrote one book in English. He said that his grandfather, Charles Green, had built his house on the edge of what had been a race course, and that in the summer when he visited, the house was "filled too with the sound of laughter."[9]

Julian Green apparently disagreed with what his sister rote about the family and some other accounts. His adopted son (Julian was never married) wrote

I am the son of Julian Green & I must answer you for him because he is in Germany. I must tell you that much information is incorrect. The narrative of Anne Green which you are using is a romantic (fictional, embellished) narrative. For example, not one photograph shows Edward at age 8, 10, 12 or 14 unkempt; on the contrary because Charles J. Green had, as you well know . . . . .and properties, in Europe as in America. He was English until his death. His children were sent to Virginia for university studies & Edward (was) in

Europe, notably in Austria, a` Stella Matutina, one of the well known Jesuit boys schools. He was born in Grove, not in Lawn. It was not a question of General Mosby, but of J.B. Stuart, the narrative was written by Julian Green from the recollectious of his father.

The third wife of Charles Green had no children.

The value (cost) of the house in Savannah was not $93,000 but Ł50,000, not counting the paintings & the statues. I have the (accountings) and the receipts of John Norris.

Finally, Charles Green, like his English family, was entirely secessionists; like the father's side of Julian Green (Hunton, Moxley, Douglas, Beauregard).

These were several lists of information I had.

With my best regard,

Jean Eric Green[10]

Green's oldest son, Benjamin, served as a Confederate officer. In a different way, Charles Green got involved himself. In the first part of the war, he and his sister, Elizabeth, Mrs. John Low, made a trip to England. There they were shadowed by U.S. detectives who followed them to Canada and to Detroit where he was arrested for carrying secret dispatches for President Davis. He was accused of "hotly espousing" the Rebel Cause. He was imprisoned for a time at Fort Warren in Boston Harbor. Green made the most of his imprisonment. (He seemed to make the most of everything.) He was much beloved by the ladies of the post who presented him with six damask napkins with "Charles Green, Fort Warren" embroidered in red cotton across one corner.[11] He claimed to be innocent, but later dispatches were delivered to Davis intact. Some said they were hidden in his boots and others that they were kept underneath Elizabeth's hair.   She was not imprisoned.

General G. Moxley Sorrel and General William W. Mackall visited at The Lawn whenever they were in the area during the war.[12]   Green was always having some kind of company. If not relatives or high-ranking officers, it would be neighbors and persons of the community. Diarist Gray said that one Saturday in August, Molly Balch, Thomas' daughter, came over to Ringwood. They were expecting the Rev. Mr. Pollock to spend the night so he wouldn't have so far to go to Greenwich to preach. She wrote on August 27, 1864 about going to church at Greenwich, but first they went by The Lawn

> to call on Mr. Bing Green. Poor fellow.
> He is but a shadow of his former self.
> Consumption has a fast hold I'm afraid. Your wife
> is so like a northern teacher I once had I can't
> admire her very much though decked with costly
> jewelry.

Bing Green was apparently Charles Green's first son, Benjamin Green, who died in 1865 soon after the visit, and the woman with all the jewelry was Isabell Stoddard Green. Probably no relation, but Ewell's mother was a Stoddard.

Green's house burned in 1924, but some of the outbuildings remain. Part of the original kitchen was incorporated into a new dwelling by a son-in-law. He replaced the original carpenter Gothic Syle with Tudor Revival Style architecture.

Shoot Abe Lincoln in the Head

Just down from The Lawn, where the present Glenkirk Road crosses Broad Run, the Boley family operated a mill. Mr. Boley owned a few slaves, but when the war began and food was hard to obtain, he freed his slaves, telling them to support themselves by going North. One of the slaves chose to remain with the Boley family. One day, a Union soldier stopped the slave who was in a Boley wagon and asked the whereabouts of a community resident named Marstellar. The slave said he had seen the man several days before and told where he could be located. Later when the slave failed to return home, the Boley family began searching for him. The unfortunate man was found the next day hanging from a tree for having divulged the whereabouts of Marstellar.

When the Union Army occupied the area around Greenwich, food was quite scarce for the people of the community as well as for the soldiers. Expecting to find something to eat around a mill, a group of Union soldiers went to the Boley farm. Philip Boley was a child 3 or 4 years old. One soldier thought the boy was cute. He sat Philip on his knee and asked, "Do you know any songs or rhymes?" Philip shook his head indicating he did not, but the soldier kept insisting.

At last Philip remembered a rhyme he had recently learned. He grinned at the soldier, and as instructed he recited, "I'll fill my musket with powder and lead, then I'll shoot Abe Lincoln in the head."

The soldier caught Philip, turned him over his knee and was ready to spank him when his sergeant caught his raised arm. "You are the one who kept insisting he tell you a rhyme. It's not his fault that you don't like the one he told you."

Many years later Philip built a house closer to Greenwich on the present Glenkirk Road. When his mother walked over the land with him, she pointed out a knoll where nothing was growing. "See that bare spot," she said. "That ground is cursed. Nothing will ever grow there because that's where the Union Army was camped." Even today, that area is still barren. All that grows there are a few weeds, said one of Philip's descendants.[13]

Come Home

The locals were weary of both sides, but especially the Yankees, camping all over their property. Diarist Jackson said the

Union forces were also tired of the guerrilla activities of Mosby and others. They were angry at the community support given to them.

August 2, 1862 Sunday afternoon. . . There is now great excitement in this & surrounding neighborhoods, General Pope, the Commander of the Northern Forces in Virginia has ordered that all of the citizens shall whither take the Oath of Allegiance to the U.S. or leave their property & go South. Tis a pretty hard trial to them to do either, though all I hear speak of it say if it does come to pass they will certainly go South and right in the Army, so I think the South will be greatly benefited. General McDowel (a Yankey officer) on being asked his opinion on the subject said he thought it would be the best thing they could do for the South. They seen to be very tired of the war on both sides & well they may be, poor things. I think the soldier's life must be a hard life indeed.

There are a great many deserting this Army above here, under Pope. They say there are almost constantly passing New Baltimore & Mr. Reid was here last week, says there were ten passed Greenwich one day. Oh! When will this horrid War end, when will we have peace again.

August 22, 1862 Friday morning. . .Four deserters came by here Sunday evening. Yesterday two came by. The Yankeys have stopped taking the citizens and making them take the Oath, I believe, though they have got several from the neighborhood of Greenwich. Mr. Reid is among them. He declared he would not take the Oath under any circumstances, and I hope he will not, though I understand his wife sent him word to take it and come home...

Balch wrote about

> the trial of seven deserters from the Federal army. It was a solemn time. The lives of six were saved, and the Maine General [Howard] exerted himself to save the seventh, but all in vain. The culprit was taken out a solitary victim, and under the fire of twelve men, he fell over into his grave in the rear of the Presbyterian Church. Not wishing to hear the fatal shot, the writer wandered away from the Manse into the very center of our densely-matted pines. What was the use, thought I, of killing that one man. To prevent desertion. Why, in his dying speech he earnestly exhorted his comrades to desert. Four or five were shot near Brandy Station, and for a week afterwards refugees from the army were streaming by my house. At all events, the culprit was launched into eternity in a moment. [14]

Charles Green didn't have Balch's reluctance and showed up for the firing squad in white gloves, umbrella, little dog and small sons.[15] In the early part of the war, the North had more trouble with deserters. Toward the end, many Southerners left for home. At the close, desertion was rampant, and the Confederate Army couldn't cope with the problem.

Gold Is Heavy

Just east of The Lawn, down present Vint Hill Road, across from Glenkirk Road, stood The Grove, The residence was the home of B.G.D. Moxley and later Lucy Douglass Moxley

33

Washington. The Greens, Moxleys, Sorrels, Laws and Mackalls had various kinds of family ties that linked them together.

Benjamin Gustavus Douglass Moxley had married a Miss Scott of Missouri and had lived there until her death. He then brought his two daughters, Elizabeth and Louisa, to The Grove, and their grandmother tended to them. Elizabeth married Andrew Low in 1859.[16] The Douglass in the Moxley family name came from B.G.D. Moxley's Mother, Elizabeth Douglass. The first B.G. Douglass was a Navy captain who lost his life trying to keep the British from taking gold belonging to the government when his ship was captured. He tied it around his waist and swam to shore. He didn't make it![17] It seems a seaman would know about heavy metal and water.

Charles Green's third wife, Aminta E. Fisher, was instrumental in the erection of the "Moxley Memorial Manse" near the Grove.[18] It still stands at 15012 Vint Hill Road but is no longer owned by Greenwich Presbyterian Church. Aminta, the granddaughter of Mrs. Gilbert Ireland Moxley (Aminta Elizabeth Douglas), made it a memorial to her grandmother. The first minister to live in the Manse was the oldtimer, The Rev. J. Royal Cooke, born five years after the Civil War.

General Ewell could have followed General A. P. Hill by these home places, but he would have had to wait. He instead turned south on the road by the church.

CHAPTER FOUR
THE LITTLE BRICK CHURCH

In 1810 Mrs. Aminta Elizabeth Moxley had lamented that she was the only Presbyterian in her Prince William neighborhood. Instead of just complaining, she began to invite people to her parlor for prayer and to hear visiting preachers. Mrs. Moxley persuaded her husband to build a log cabin for an assembly on their farm. The resulting building stood on the corner of the present Greenwich and Vint Hill Roads. The deacons later laid off a cemetery nearby, and over a period of years a number of persons have been buried beneath its markers. Some of these are now anonymous since the markers cannot be read. At least one has only a wooden slab with its writing long worn off. Mrs. Moxley was the first person buried in the cemetery in 1858.[1]

Reverend Thomas Balch wrote about the kirk, the center of Greenwich.

> There were two Churches in Greenwich-
> one Free, and the other Presbyterian. The Free was
> of plank, and the other of brick. The plank one
> perished in the war; but the brick is still standing a
> monument of religious taste, and uninjured in the
> hurricane of civic strife. [2]

He may have meant that another congregation used the old log building.

Ma Has A Headache

Charles Green became very much interested in the local church and soon proved to be its foremost patron. The Greens purchased the present-day church site which bordered on the old location. They donated and solicited money for the construction of the brick building which was completed in 1858. Mrs. Moxley survived to see her dream realized but died the same year at the age of 83.

Green and the congregation chose to build the church building in the only Rusticated Gothic Revival style of architecture in the county.[3] They also caused several stiles of English fashion to be built in the fence-line for alighting with ease from carriages, whatever the weather. The interesting looking gazebo-like structures and the hooded entrances for the sanctuary of similar fashion are still in place. The church yard and cemetery had to be fenced in order to keep out nearby cattle and other domestic animals. Some of these may have been Green's sheep. The building and cemetery are now registered as Prince William County and Virginia State Historic Landmarks.

Diarist Gray noted when the building was completed. "Saturday morning, July 31, 1858. Ma has a headache this morning so we are not going to Greenwich to the dedication of the new church."

English Property

Green took care of church property as well as his own. During the War, soldiers from both sides built campfires on the Greenwich churchyard and in nearby woods. A number of White Oaks, a few over 200 years old, still stand around the church. What tales these trees overheard. Federals with their usual disrespect for sanctuaries threatened to take over the brick building as a hospital, or possibly as a stable, as in some places, at the time of the two battles of Manassas. They were put off by the threats of Green who had stipulated that if the property was used for any other purpose it would revert to the donor. He told them this "would make it English property as I am an Englishman."[4] Federals didn't want to antagonize the British when they were courting England to stay neutral so they left the building alone. They used the former sanctuary, the second house of logs, which still stood at that time, but burned shortly afterwards.

As Ewell moved through Greenwich he could not help but see the Greenwich Presbyterian Church in the grove of White Oak trees just across from the west side of The Lawn. He knew that portions of French's Third Corps had camped all over and around the grounds the day before. Ewell was not a Presbyterian, though his brother William had become a Presbyterian minister, if a somewhat eccentric one. Ewell knew of many of the church members as well as some of it's ministers. At one time he had declared that he despised rigid and pious Presbyterians. "Sour Presbyterians," he had call them.[5] At any rate, he gave evidence of respecting these people.

A Dangerous Spy

Services at the church had become very irregular and spasmodic during the war. The brick church building which replaced the original log structure appeared to still be in good shape on October 14, 1863. The minister at the beginning of the War had been Rev. John W. Pugh. Diarist Gray wrote November 3, 1861 that she went to Greenwich to hear Mr. Pugh preach from Hebrews 12-16. Greenwich was linked with Warrenton Presbyterian for Pugh's services, and there was only one Session of Elders.

Pugh also served in the Southern Army. A reserve corps of Warrenton citizens was known as the Rev. J.W. Pugh's Lee Guards.[6] Susan E. Caldwell wrote to her Papa, "I wonder who will be captain now. Lieut. Pugh is very unpopular so it is said."[7] A citizen of Warrenton noted that "Mr. Pugh is still a Prisoner in Washington taken while here by the Yankey Army."[8] When former Old School Presbyterian colleagues of his, now on the other side, heard that he was imprisoned as a dangerous spy, many put away politics and visited him in Capitol Prison.[9] Incarcerated, Pugh would not have been either in Warrenton or Greenwich when Ewell rode through.

On March 16, 1863, The Reverend Mr. Pugh was assigned chaplain of the 41st Virginia Infantry at $50 per month.[10] He retained the position until April 1865. After the war, The Rev. Mr. Pugh moved north and took churches in Indiana and Illinois which seems strange for such an ardent Rebel. He died in 1912.

Something of a Tease

Diarist Gray revealed that church attendance had attractions for Ringwood girls other than long discourses. She also noted on February 19, 1865 another preacher who on occasion gave a good sermon, one Dr. Pollock. That day snow was on the ground, and they went in an ox-drawn sleigh. The Reverend Doctor Abraham David Pollock, III, had been a Presbyterian minister in Pennsylvania before coming to Virginia. He had a reputation for burning eloquence and stood a stately figure. It wasn't hard for him to win the hand and fortune of Miss Lizzie Lee, a local beauty and heiress. Two sons and three daughters were born to their union. The elder son, Inspector General of Pickett's Division, was killed in the charge at Gettysburg. Their daughters were known in the area as the "Three Graces."

Daughter "Bert" gained some fame in helping thwart the capture of Mosby. She overheard the conversation of a servant who tattled to the Union troops. She bribed her way into Union headquarters in Warrenton to get more information and then rode in a storm at night through many dangers to give the alarm.[11]

The Rev. Dr. Pollock was something of a tease. Once Mrs. Pollock, a daughter of Charles Lee, Attorney General to Washington and Adams, packed his bag to go to a presbytery meeting. She told him to wear a clean shirt each day. He returned wearing all five shirts at the same time. He lived in Warrenton until he died May 3, 1890.[12]

A Large Funeral

The Reverend Thomas Balch often preached at Greenwich. Once he planned a special event. Gray wrote on April 19, 1862 that Balch planned to conduct a funeral service at Greenwich for all the soldiers of the counties of Fauquier and Prince William. She felt that many would have attended, and that it would have been a great occasion. But Union officers got angry and stopped it.

On April 19, Aunt Belle had written to Gray that some members of the Prince William Calvary had gotten cut off from their company, and that the Yankees were coming up the railroad; many were at Catlett. She called on God for the strength to endure and his love to give hope that he was still with them. She noted, "The Yankees found Mr. Balch's notice [about the special service] and tore it up. They are expected at Greenwich tomorrow, so will be no service."

A Big Meeting

The community life centered around its churches. Opportunities for social relationships and relaxation made the Sabbath a happy time. Some of the girls at Ringwood were serious and tried to be "consistent Christians," a term popular at that time. A religion revival occurred during the war touching troops and civilians. Numbers of persons attended more than one church service as opportunities presented themselves. Camp meetings were popular as Jackson indicated.

July 16, 1860. Papa took Cattie & I to New Baltimore on the 7th of the month. We intended to come back on the 8th but there was a big meeting going on so I staid and came home on the 14th. Mr. Florance brought me home. We went to the Branch yesterday it was class meeting day. I stayed at New Baltimore eight days and heard fifteen sermons, six was preached by Mr. Thomas, one by Mr. Newman & eight by Mr. Biddings of Alexandria. He is an excellent preacher. They are what is called New School Baptist, but I can see very little difference in them and the Methodists the greatest difference is in their

Communion, they preach the very same doctring...I wish I could remember them all, I ought to have written them down.

General Ewell had been reared in an Episcopalian influence, perhaps one reason he thought Presbyterians dour, but he had not joined a church. In the Shenandoah Valley Campaign, the General walked over to the tent of Stonewall Jackson before a battle. He heard Jackson praying aloud for guidance and did not enter. The prayer was so devout and beautiful that for the first time he felt an urge to become a Christian, Ewell later reported. The Reverend Moses Drury Hogge, a close friend of the family, had a role in Ewell's spiritual growth. His wife Lizinka was also influential in his making a profession. After his leg healed from his amputation, and he returned to command, he met with spiritual leaders to discuss ways to proclaim the gospel to the soldiers. Lizinka and Hogge worked together to help the General overcome his worst habit. In the army he swore with elegance and was able to curse in a manner beyond description. As he sought serious commitment, he began to bridle his tongue. Occasionally under stress, he lapsed into former ways.[13] Trying to march his troops through the narrow roads of Greenwich, already clogged with General A. P. Hill's men, stressed him considerably.

CHAPTER FIVE
PRINCE WILLIAM MUD

A Spooky Place

When Ewell got to Greenwich, he was very much upset to find General A. P. Hill's troops, which had come from New Baltimore, passing through. Rather than wait for Hill to clear the lane, he decided to take a back way. At the church, he turned down now Burwell Road, between the church and The Lawn, toward the site of Baileysburg, just south of Greenwich.

In the early 19th century, Carr Bailey owned a thousand acre plantation on the corner of Burwell Road and Edwards, now Owl's Nest Road. His Mansion House, which was located at the end of the present Hopkins Lane, burned in the early 1920's; perhaps other buildings went up in flames also. Being very close to the larger town of Greenwich, Baileysburg expired with Mr. Bailey in the 1850's.[1]

The Edmond family lived near this site.[2] In the church cemetery, a monument lists J. B. who died in 1862 age 22; S. I. who died the same year at 20; A. L. who died in 1863, age 13 and T. E., killed in the Battle of Seven pines 1862, 23 years of age. It was a tough time for the Edmondses.

Newman Hopkins, who lived near the house site, said he remembered an ancient barn in the neighborhood. As a youngster, he was afraid to go by it. Local people said that old man Edmonds had hanged himself, and his ghost lived there.[3] It is not clear what the relationship of these Edmonds is to the ones in Gray's diary, but she mentions several persons with that name.

Just south of Baileysburg, on Burwell Road, the Weaver plantation was situated. In 1724 Colonel Charles Carter owned it. By 1857 it belonged to Christiana Eleanor Weaver. Part of the house was incorporated into another structure and still stands. Family members of later occupants tell about Caleb, a Confederate soldier. The girl he was going to marry lived in the house but died. Caleb was wounded in the war and also died. Some local residents claim that he comes back to the dwelling looking for his fiance. If a visitor to the premises sits by the house long enough, the ghost of Caleb appears, they say.[4] A spooky neighborhood!

Ewell turned east at the corner, heading towards Bristoe, trying to make up for lost time. It was going to be back roads, farm fields and woods, but he knew the way. Perhaps he had forgotten it had been a wet season. Maybe he no longer remembered what happened when it rained. Samuel J. Martin accuses Ewell of being too conservative and timid and said he had plodded along on the way to Bristoe.[5] But fighting at Auburn had delayed Ewell about four hours already, and at this point A. P. Hill's troops were in his path. He did the best he could, but what he encountered on the way was "Prince William mud, oh Lud." An explanation for Black Jack soils in Prince William County, though not necessarily in this particular area, seems appropriate. The Reverend Dr. Pollock, who sometimes preached at Greenwich, is supposed to have described it at Old Possum Ford across Rock Branch as, "So wet in winter, it never leaked, and so dry in summer that you can't drive a nail into it without greasing."[6]

Hardly Puny

After General Ewell made his turn towards Bristoe, it was not long before he marched through the backside of the farm of Michael and Harriet House. Michael had come over from Holland with his family. His father and half the shipload had died on the voyage. Michael had one son, Nathaniel. An obituary of Nathaniel in 1901 reads

> Their son, Nathaniel was a worthy scion of the parent stock. He was of an exceedingly fragile organism. Such was his native pluck and energy that he successfully met and discharged as many of life's arduous duties and labors as any one who is

blessed with full physical vigor. I did not meet him during the four years of civil strife, but I have been credibly informed that there was no man in the Army of Northern Virginia who rendered more constant and consistent service than Nathaniel House, and he was recognized at headquarters as among the best of General Lee's couriers.[7]

Not only was Nathaniel a soldier, but after his first wife died, he took another. In all he had eleven children. He lived to be 72. Hardly puny! He and his wives are buried at Greenwich Presbyterian Church cemetery as well as numbers of others of the family.

It Still Stands

It didn't take General Ewell and his Corps long to get close to home ground. Soon he made out The Manse, the then current home of the Reverend Thomas Balch, which still stands at 10214 Lonesome Road. Apparently Thomas had bought the land from Western Smallwood or his heirs during the period 1860 - 1865 when few deeds were recorded or those filed were lost. The county government accepted his title at the close of hostilities, but he later had to go to court over the title. The Union army had not harmed it as Balch wrote.

But the question may be asked. . .was your Manse injured by the war? No; from the last advices it is still erect. Its bees are still riding on their chariot plants, its birds are still twittering from its locust boughs, and its grassy knolls have not been stained by a drop of blood. My books are intact.[8]

Balch was a small man, which surprised one of the visitors to his manse. The guest asked how much he weighed, and the

Reverend replied, "99 3/4 lbs."[9] He showed a Major Jones a "large picture of my small self."[10] He didn't seem to care too much about his appearance and during the war ran out of shoes and other garments. Several officers sent him shoes. The war years and emancipation of the slaves may have left him financially strapped.

During the War he celebrated his 70th birthday. On that occasion the family and friends put on a tableau and served coffee which was very scarce. He enjoyed the "Java" but had some other drink in mind.

> But, said I, did not Ella Edmonds, the rebel and Sarah Ruby, the Union, each send me a bottle of blackberry wine? They did, but they are locked up, said the lady of the Manse, who is great on temperance. Blackberries can never prevent a man from counting the horns of the moon. Didn't Mr. Osmyn, from Jersey, send me four bottles, and Charlotte Mitchell three, and Irene Leach two, and Mrs. Green five. . . It is my wish to drink the health of Gen. Lee. Then your politics will be known. No, my politics are not pinned to the sleeve of Gen. Lee, but he is your cousin. Whilst he was a captain, we never heard you claim kin with him; but now its counsin Lee.[11]

Balch lived to be 85. His wife, Susan Carter of the distinguished Virginia Carter family, was about eight years his junior.

Thomas Balch probably was an Old School Presbyterian and generally pious. He remarked

> The first battle of Manassas was fought on a Sabbath. We wish that men-at-arms would choose some other day for their sanguinary work..My Hermitage was full of refugees. Mrs. Commodore Jones, of Sharon, was one of them,

44

whose delicate health made her exceedingly nervous. The drama was opened early in the morning of that brilliant day in July, 1861. A neighbor rode by my house in great haste, with a spy-glass fastened on his shoulder, through which to peer at the combatants. Well: if it had been Wednesday your correspondent would have staid at home, but being the one which was kept holy in Eden. . .he took his Bible and spent the sacred hours between sunrise and sunset in reading of Patriarchs, Prophets, Apostles, Martyrs, and of Him who is Lord of all. That Bible must be handed down to some one as an heirloom. It was presented to its owner by the Christian ladies of Greenwich Church. . .About sunset my Bible closed. It was time for our evening meal.[12]

Balch was a man of peace as Julia Ringwood told Federal General Newton when her father sent her to the officer to ask for coffee. Balch dramatized the meeting as he wrote

Do you know, said the General, that but yester-night, Moseby made a dash on our camp and stole fourteen horses. We have so heard, said the Roman Julia. . .when that was done, we who live at the Manse were asleep in our hammocks. Your father, you say, is above the military age. Long ago, General, long ago; but were he young as Adam before his fall, he would not in nine hundred years engage in war. He is not an Esau roaming in quest of game, but a plain man dwelling in tents, and like Isaac, he often goes forth to meditate at evening-tide. Is the old man well? said the General. Quite hale and hearty. He can still walk off his five miles; but sends me because no Knight of La

Mancha can deny a few berries to a lady. But don't you harbor Mosby?   No General.[13]

The Reverend believed the writer more effective than the warrior.   General Meade gave one of his daughters an officer escort to get home.   Two Confederate soldiers captured him despite her protests. Balch penned a letter to Honorable James A. Sheldon, Secretary of War, who ordered his release from the Richmond prison.[14]

Again he proved the power of the pen. Sometime during the war, a party of Union cavalry carried off two of Thomas' horses.   He sent their commanding officer a letter eventually printed in the *Presbyterian* newspaper in Philadelphia during the war.   It found its way in the pages of Richmond's *Central Presbyterian* some seven months after the surrender.

> Colonel: Yesterday a squad of your men took off a couple of my horses. One of them is cream-coloured, like the steed that Washington rode at Yorktown in 1781, and the other a bright sorrel, like one mentioned in the "Arabian Nights." Please consult Blackstone on the mighty difference between *meum* and *tuum*. Possession is nine out of the twelve points of the law, and therefore you have no moral or military right to Fan and Reuben. It is not my purpose to use either of them in making a raid on your camp. --A Presbyterian minister must not turn soldier, as if he were a Romish Pontiff. One of the animals is a pony, that carries my corn and wheat to Langley's Mill, and you must not forget that Henry Clay was a mill-boy. With the going down of the sun, let me see both my steeds in their own fragrant clover-fields, and the vesper beams of the day will reflect renewed lustre on your deeds. Permit me to subscribe my middle name, in the hope that your

sense of justice will be in full flower. Thomas
Bloomer Balch.[15]

Apparently he got them back.
Balch was a Southern sympathizer, but that didn't keep him
from opening his doors to others.

> The solitude of the Manse became
> enlivened by strangers. . .Two thousand in all
> though not at one and same time. They came in
> groups. Many humorous and some tragic incidents
> took place; but the former might be inappropriate
> to an ecclesiastical journal. To some of the soldiers
> we presented a variety of religious tracts, which
> were courteously received. They promised to give
> them a faithful reading. Sometimes my consort
> would, of a Sabbath evening, go in where they
> were, read and explain a chapter in the Bible, and
> then kneel down and pray for them and all whom
> they had left at home. They showed deep feeling.[16]

Mrs. Balch said, "And my creed is that the rites of
hospitality are more sacred than the laws of war."[17] Mackall
related that during the Civil War Mr. Balch, although a Southerner
in his feelings, prayed so earnestly for Northern soldiers every time
they came to the house, that he was able to get anything he wanted
from them. He even got real coffee when his neighbors were
compelled to use beans for that purpose. His wife was also of a
very religious temperament and great in prayer. She would begin
with a room full of officers and pray on and on until there would
be no one left but herself. In that way she saved the corn and hay
from being taken by them.[18]
Even Mosby stopped by The Manse.

> We are indebted to the loss of his way for
> a visit from the celebrated Major Moseby. He

called about nine o'clock at night and dismounted under some locust trees before the door of the Manse. A full moon was shining, but the shade of the trees prevented me from a good view of his contour.[19]

Balch made both pastoral and social calls on persons in the community. Diarist Jackson, January 25, 1864, wrote that "Mr. Billie Wise & Mr. A. Marsterla...and Mr. Balch spent the night with us last night. Mr. Balch calls very often, an English gentleman by the name of Alston has also been here several times."

The several children of Balch were already grown at the time of the war. At one point a neighbor warned the minister that the Yankee soldiers were going to arrest him, likely because he had so many persons coming and coming from his place. They also suspected his sons. When an Union officer approached him and asked him about his family, he replied,

> Yes, Mary Landon and Julia Ringwood are from home. My son, William Cowper, is in the Black Horse, and my other sons, Charles Carter and Robert Monro, are in Forrest's Legion, to the Southwest. But hope you will both dine with me, and you will then see the lady of the Manse, a person worth seeing. Understand, Lieutenant, that you are the arresting officer. Just so, he replied, and it is a most unpleasant office, but a soldier is obliged to obey his orders.[20]

One of the sons was later arrested.

> On the morning that Gen. Ewell left for the war, the writer went over to his residence to bid him adieu. It was a distance of five hundred yards from my own dwelling. His brother committed the diminutive creature [his dog] to the keeping of my

son, and a remarkable attachment grew up between the parties. His temporary owner could not stroll to my gate without being accompanied by the dog. He followed him wherever he went, and was with him on the evening he was captured and taken to Washington. Bruto returned after night, and we concluded that his master would soon make his appearance. But he did not, for he was safely lodged in the Carroll House. The dog was disconsolate, and for several days refused everykind of nourishment, constantly looking in the direction where his master was taken. When the prisoner returned the canine affair could not suppress its joy.[21]

He and his wife also cared for the hurt of either side. A Mississippi soldier was brought to their home after being wounded. The family tended him, but he died and was buried in a clump of cherry trees near The Manse.[22]

In the first engagement at Bristoe, around the time of the Second Battle of Manassas, Balch went to the battlefield. He said, "Visited Bristoe, which is four miles from the Manse, where soldiers were laying, who were wounded in the skirmish between Ewell and Hooker. It was a mournful sight."[23]

He conducted a number of funerals. He participated in the service for the fallen Hoskins, the English soldier who rode with Mosby. "We laid him down in the cemetery of the village, [Greenwich Presbyterian] and his father has sent over funds to rear a neat tablet to his memory."[24] Grief struck his family. Diarist Jackson wrote June 13, 1864, "Miss Lizzie and I went down to Mr. Balch's yesterday to hear him preach the funeral sermon of his daughter, Mrs. E. Carter, who died in Alabama. She was highly esteemed by all who knew her."

During the war years, Balch on occasion conducted Sabbath morning worship at Greenwich. He also preached during the first of the war for a group of Presbyterians sympathetic to the

North, but who later abandoned their church and went across the Mason Dixon Line. He conducted a regular worship service in his home during the war, inviting men of either side to attend, of course at different times.[25]

From his front porch, Balch could see General Ewell's place, called Stoney Lonesome. During the April snowstorm in 1863, Union Provost Marshall Leslie was staying at Balch's house. "Leslie very kindly took an ambulance and brought the General's books to my house. They were preserved in that way, for some soldiers think no more of Homer's Iliad than of the History of Tom Thumb..."[26]

A Lonesome Place

As he approached Bristoe, General Ewell could see his old home, Stoney Lonesome, as well as Balch's Manse. It was so named because the ground was rocky and the site isolated. Ewell had been born in Georgetown. His father, a physician, died, and the family had to give up its Centreville home and move out further into the country on Ewell property. In 1820 the tract contained approximately 1,300 acres. In 1850 the place contained 480 acres which were worth about $5.00 per acre. The family at that time grew wheat, corn, Irish potatoes, hay and raised horses, cows, oxen, cattle, sheep and swine.[27] In 1850 there were 4 slaves. In 1860 only two show up in the Prince William Slave Schedule.[28]

Elizabeth Stoddert Ewell, Richard's mother, possessed lots of courage and determination. She had moved from luxury in Georgetown to a hard life without much complaint. She accepted little help from wealthier family members. She taught a little school and tried to farm and managed to survive.[29]

After Richard finished West Point, he had entered the U.S. Army, spending much of the time in the West. He often spoke of the farm and his home. Whenever he did get home, it seemed he was recuperating from illness. Once taking a coach from Richmond to Stony Lonesome he came down with a chill and had to stop for the night at a neighbor's in Greenwich. The next day,

New Year's Eve, his family came to get him and put him to bed.[30]

Ewell had a mania for farming, and if the War had not intervened, he felt he would likely have owned and made Stoney Lonesome a place proud to visit.[31] Anyway, he continued his interest in Stoney Lonesome. His mother no longer lived there, having moved and then died a few years earlier.

The house and farm did not seem to have a regular tenant during the War. At favorable times, Ewell, family or friends, civilian and army, might take lodging. General Johnston may have stayed one night on route, and William Ewell gave him a fine bottle of Madeira wine to drink.[32] The Confederates and probably the Union Army camped in and around the house. Thomas Balch sometimes went over to visit them there.[33]

Ewell didn't want the old home to be destroyed by the Yankees and the furniture and mementos of the past to be profaned by the invaders. He would rather that they burn the property. In fact, his brother William had wanted to do so himself, and Ewell later concluded that it would have been better to have torched it.[34] Actually, Richard no longer held any title to the farm for he sold his share to his brother, William, in 1850. Still he frequented the place and had great affection and concern for it.

The General would like to have stopped to check out the premises. He didn't have time for he was already behind schedule. It was getting towards sunset. He knew that the property had run down some, though it was in better shape than most in the region. Just recently a neighbor had told the General the house was standing and, while in poor condition, that the fences had not been burned. Movable furniture had been made safe elsewhere. While the sheep had all been slaughtered, most of the other livestock still lived. Union soldiers had vandalized the place and taken many items including the fine books and some letters written by Thomas Jefferson. (Maybe Balch had them.) The family had buried the china to hide it.[35] Ewell kept his eyes on his old home place as long as he could, but the increasing sound of cannonading and noise of musket and rifle fire urged him on towards Bristoe.

CHAPTER SIX
A GLOOMY SCENE

A Bloody Battle

About 4:00 PM, General Lee and Early's division arrived at the Bristoe area and discovered a battle in progress. Ewell and his corps soon appeared and formed on the west side of A. P. Hill's line of battle. A. P. Hill had arrived earlier and tried to keep Meade's troops from crossing Broad Run. Stuart's Cavalry had not been out in front of Hill, and Hill did not know what lay ahead. He attacked anyway. Union Major General Gouverneur Kemble Warren, coming up the railroad from Catlett, struck down what looked like a victory for Hill. Warren and Hill had been surprised to meet. Both saw at once the advantage of the railroad embankment. Warren hollered out to his Irish brigade, "Run for the cutting" and beat the Confederates to the position.[1]

Warren was the famous "Savior of Little Round Top" at Gettysburg for which he had gotten a lot of glory, and at the age of 33 he was famous. After the battle at Bristoe, he boasted to his fellow officers that he had whipped the Rebs pretty good. And he had. In a few minutes, Heth's Confederate Division lost 1,161 men, 20 percent of its muster. The Rebels were rallying, but evening fell, and in the darkness the Union Army escaped over Broad Run towards Washington, D.C. The Union artillery continued to shell after dark. After the gunfire ended, both sides heard the cries of the fallen. It started to rain, and showers fell on the wounded.

A Mournful Look

Jacksie who lived near Brentsville, wrote on October 15, 1863, "Ben left this morning to join his company. He thinks it is

52

near Greenwich. They were fighting all around the house yesterday."

Portions of the Confederate infantry stayed on rain-soaked fields around Bristoe through most of Thursday, October 15. Lee, Hill and Ewell rode around the battlefield covered with dead soldiers. A Confederate soldier, William W. Chamberlain, remembered fifty years later the mournful look on Lee's face. He also vividly recalled Ewell's bald head with gray hair on the back.[2]

A battle-fatigued sergeant from the Twenty-seventh North Carolina complained to his major that his rifle had kicked so much the day before that his shoulder was almost useless. The officer seeing a bloody hole in the infantryman's uniform at the shoulder asked him if he hadn't been shot.

The poor land of the battle area was covered with a growth of small pines, other scrubby trees, wire grass and broom straw, but there were a lot of rabbits good for sport and eating, noticed one soldier.[3] After the battle the countryside seemed gloomier then it had already been. Only a few chimneys marked where houses had stood.

Lee put the Second Corps to work destroying the railroad and began his retreat behind the Rappidan. General Ewell took time to visit Stoney Lonesome. He found windows broken, fences burned and further vandalization of the place. He dug up the hidden family china and found two or three chairs in good enough condition to take with him.[4]

Yester Years

In 1883, Michael G. Early bought Stoney Lonesome and changed its dark name to East View, perhaps to brighten his environment.[5] Nothing remains of the dwelling, but current owners of the land call it Stoney Lonesome Farm.

No family descendants live in the area, but traces of yester years remain. On the present Reid Lane, past the bridge over Kettle Run, on top of a wooded knoll on the west side, not far from Stoney Lonesome, stands a tombstone which reads, Benjamin

Douglas, Born 1743, Died 1827. On another side of the same stone the inscription, Sophia Douglas Euell, is written.

Another Ewell, Sarah is buried at Greenwich along side A. B. Carrington. The Rev. Alexander B. Carrington, a chaplain in the Confederacy, entered as a private in the ranks and after the War ministered at Greenwich.[6] He married for his second wife, Sarah Ewell, daughter of Colonel James B. Ewell who is also buried at Greenwich. She was born at Greenville, the early Ewell homestead, near the site of the tombstone just referred to. After the war, Colonel Ewell went to Texas a while and then returned to live with his daughter and The Rev. Mr. Carrington at Greenwich. He drilled for oil near Cedar Run and Double Poplars Road. He got water instead, which still runs out of the casing said James Cooke. The site is near Route 2, Box 201 Catlett.

A 345 foot high point east of Kettle Run and south of Fitzwater Drive is named Ewell's Hill. Just down stream from where the present Lonesome Road crosses Kettle Run appear remains of a mill site on the former Ewell land.

On October 15, 1863, General Ewell didn't have time to think about family presence in Prince William. He ordered his men to keep busy before they rejoined Lee.

Nary a Reb

Amanda Edmonds who lived in upper Fauquier had lots of time to reflect on October 15.

> All the Rebs leave this morning. John [Hatcher] first bids us a long goodbye to join the gallant old Eighth. The rest come in and with a goodbye and lunch, set sail to join their daring commander, Major Mosby, at Middleburg. Every man is required to be at his post today. I hope he will have a brilliant haul this time. Oh! I have been so lonesome all day with "nary" a Reb. This evening Mrs. Carter came and alleviated the

loneliness in a measure. I have become perfectly devoted to the society of the Rebels, too much so for my own happiness and too indifferent to females. Why should I not love them for their heroic valor and fortitude and some very pleasant, agreeable and fine company. I can look back when the war is over and recall some of the happiest moments of my life - yes, even amid the terrible war with all its sorrow and grief. I have spent many happy days full of change, variety and romance - excitement is the thing that suits my fancy.[7]

The Facts Speak

Ewell must have had enough excitement. He shared in the fault for the defeat at Bristoe. Hill admitted it was his error, but he said if he had waited and missed an opportunity he would have blamed himself likewise (and so would others). Ewell said little, determined to let the facts speak for themselves.

Ewell had gone to war because he was from Virginia, risking everything because of it. Towards the end, the strain of battle began to further tell on him. Around Richmond, in the close, he was relieved of his command and assigned to a desk in the city. (General Warren, who came apart later, was also relieved and remained bitter all his life.) Right at the end Ewell was again put over troops. He was captured at Sailer Creek and sent to prison at Fort Warren in Boston Harbor, the same place the Union confined Charles Green.

Some criticized Ewell because he seemed over concerned to protect his wife Lizinka's belongings in Tennessee. Others claimed he was in too big a hurry to make peace. Even though Ewell had a good record, many did not consider that he had been a successful commander. Some felt he lacked the decision necessary as a commander. Donald C. Pfanz disagreed and said that he was as good as any other in the Army of Northern Virginia and better than most.[8]

While he had been at Ft. Warren, Ewell may have begun to remember Stephen McCormick's invention and to think more and more that it was time for the South to "beat its swords into plowshares" (Isaiah 2:4). When he was released after 3 months, he considered settling near Williamsburg, but since his wife, Lizinka, had much property in Tennessee, they chose that state. He did well. He took his wife's run down holdings, and in three years he made it a first class stock farm. He also leased a plantation in Mississippi and prospered. He died at Spring Hill, Tennessee, January 25, 1872 at the age of 55.

By the end of the war, Ewell may or may not have agreed with Balch that the pen is more powerful than the sword. Later, remembering the youthful times in Prince William, Virginia and the more successful mature years in Tennessee, he may have voted for the plow as the most potent of all.

Part Two

More About Persons And Places Along The Way

CHAPTER SEVEN
THE BARONESS AND ROGUE'S ROAD

Baroness Frederick Riedesel, her children and several servants, traveled through Old Prince William in January of 1779. Her husband, General Reidesel, commanded the Brunswick Hessians troop that had fought with the British at the Battle of Saratoga. They were captured by Americans, and some time after their defeat the prisoners were marched south to Charlottesville.

The party entered Virginia by crossing the Potomac River below Point of Rocks at Norman's Ford. Ice jams made the passage dangerous. They then moved towards Leesburg. Thomas Anburey, a lieutenant in Burgoyne's army, mapped the journey along the Old Carolina Road.

Iroquois Indians and wild animals, traveling the line of least resistance, had carved the Old Carolina footpath from Maryland into Carolina out of wilderness. Settlers and traders fought the red men and turned it into a road. Thieves and cut-throats also frequented it and made the trips perilous. For this reason, travelers also called it Rogues's Road.

"In those days, road was a vague and sometimes abstract point of view," said Fairfax Harrison.[1] Thoroughfares were often more or less open tracks through fields. If after bad weather the ruts were unclear, journeymen had the right to ride horses or wagons over the edges of planters' corn. Farmers could even put gates across the right of way. Sometimes persons had trouble telling where Carolina Road began and ended. George Washington got lost on Rogues Road in 1784 and had to follow his compass from Norman's Ford to Prince William Old Court House.

A Break-Neck Road

The Baroness said they were often in danger of their lives along this break-neck road. She was also frightened by the wild country. The party suffered from the weather. Snow encrusted the road, but the surface was not hard enough to bear the weight of the travelers who kept sinking up to their knees and cutting their shins on the ice.

According to Anburey, they made their first camp near Goose Creek at the place now known as Evergreen Mill. (It may have been Oatland Mill.) The prisoners remained in camp here for about eight days while stragglers caught up with the main party.

When they continued their trip along the road, they came to the site of Haymarket. Here the Old Upper Dumfries Road crossed the Carolina Road. A number of years later an acquaintance of the Baroness, another European soldier, General Lafayette, French hero for the Americans, moved through the town in the opposite direction. He went on up the Carolina Road to visit ex-President Monroe at Oakhill. The way was lined with spectators who had come great distances to cheer him on. The Baroness had entertained Lafayette for a meal in her home before her forced march.

From Haymarket the group moved on across what is now Lee Highway (U.S. Route 29) and under what is now Lake Manassas before arriving at sleepy little Greenwich, a hamlet which had taken shape in the late 1700's. At the intersection of Burwell and Vint Hill Roads, stands the quaint brick Greenwich Presbyterian Church, built in 1858. Presbyterians gathered for worship in a log structure near this intersection shortly after the Baroness rode by. A Prince William Historic Marker in front of the church testifies to the passing of the Hessians.

Mad Dog Wayne

The sign in front of Greenwich Church also notes another Revolutionary War general. Anthony Wayne, it says, marched a brigade of the Pennsylvania Line through the village on the way to Yorktown. Five months earlier these soldiers had turned their guns on Wayne and his staff, walked out of the American lines to Princeton and negotiated with Congress for back pay.

In the end officers put down the mutiny. They disbanded the outfit and mustered a new group composed of many of the same men to take its place. In May of 1781, Wayne thought he detected another insurrection. He tried three soldiers and a couple of deserters and then shot them all at close range by firing squad.

Shortly afterwards, Wayne marched the brigade down the Old Carolina Road southward. Rain fell in torrents, and mud delayed movement. Four men were drowned crossing the Potomac. The General drove them mercilessly from dawn until dark attempting to walk the rebellious spirit out of them. He even advanced reveille each morning to speed them up. The troops could not be hurried, but by the time they reached Yorktown they were ready to fight.

The Baroness moved southwest from Greenwich in a straight line to Oak Dale Baptist Church says James Cook, local historian. She reversed General Ewell's march. She soon passed the present site of the recent Vint Hill Station, Army Communication Post. Not long ago this site remained the only living testimony to a history of military movement in the area. At that period one could still hear reveille and taps, even if electronically produced, while riding by.

If by this time there had been some relief in the weather, the Baroness and her party may have had trouble crossing a low spot near the old south gate at Vint Hill. Mrs. Kay Wood Beach, who once lived on a portion of the way now called Rogues Road, recalls this bog. Planked portions attempted to deal with the mud. In winter, Model A Fords had trouble driving it. In the morning, if the road was icy, autos slipped off, and if by afternoon it had thawed, more than likely travelers got stuck.[2]

Anburey noted a second camp at what is now called Auburn, located where the Lower Dumfries Road crossed Carolina Road. The Baroness may have found a night's sleep at George Neavil's Ordinary which had been built around 1740. George Washington lodged there in 1748 on one of his surveying trips. She would have noted Neavil's Mill which was restored in 1962. She would not have foreseen or even cared about hostilities between Northern and Southern troops around nearby Cedar Creek shortly before the Yankees defeated A. P. Hill at Bristoe.

The party camped next to where the Old Carolina Road crossed Marsh Road near Bealeton. The Rev. John Frederick Reichel passed through the site on returning from a missionary trip to the Bretheren in America in 1780. He reported that the Old Carolina Road was swarming with American soldiers fleeing Carolina. They had been impressed into the army but had gotten away. In addition, there were numbers of civilians from the Carolinas who were hurrying northward after the capture of Charleston.

Nothing for Dogs

After the Marsh Camp, the party crossed the Rappahannock River near Remington. The Baroness said that they had run out of food when they were only a days journey from their destination of Colle. A countryman they met on the Carolina Road gave them some acrid fruits. At noon of that day, she stopped to beg something to eat from a local woman who refused with hard words: There was "nothing for dogs of Royalists." Baroness asked for some corn meal. The woman answered, "No, that is for our Negroes, who work for us, but you have wished to kill us." Captain Edmonston offered her two guineas, but the hostile woman said, "Not for a hundred would I give you any, and should you all die of hunger it will be so much the better."[3]

At Charlottesville the Hessians, who had considerable freedom, soon made the best of their imprisonment. The Baroness did not think highly of the morals of the local people. She said the Virginians were generally inert and though blaming their laziness on the hot climate would "on the slightest inducement, in a twinkling leap up and dance about."[4] She also was critical of the practice of slavery.

After several months, General Riedesel was exchanged, and eventually the family returned home. The Baroness survived her husband by eight years and died in 1808 at the age of 62. Her portrait shows a lovely woman, and her memoirs reveal a hardy one.

The Old Carolina Road did not long remain an important thoroughfare. Changing conditions, population shifts and the coming railroads diverted much traffic elsewhere. However, with the use of county maps and a little patience, one may follow Baroness Riedesel through the Greenwich area and Old Prince William.

(From Norman's Ford, highway numbers are 660, 662, 15, 621, 625, 860, 15, 604, 602, interruption, 655, 654 to Rappahanock.)

CHAPTER EIGHT
THE PECULIAR INSTITUTION

James Cooke, local historian, recalls "Uncle" Lias Brooks who had been a slave and servant of the Greens and Veeders in Greenwich, Virginia. As a boy Cooke remembers that the old Negro liked to tell a story of his sitting on a fence during a Civil War battle. A cannon ball hit the top rail and knocked him off. He didn't say whether it was a Rebel or Yankee missile. "Uncle" Lias lived to be one of the last remaining emancipated slaves in the community. There is a picture of black Brooks among a group of white men on the porch of the old Wood's store in Greenwich.[1]

At the time of the Civil War, the majority of slaves lived in tidewater and coastal areas and in the deep South. Many slaves were owned by rich planters. Yeoman farmers and others had smaller numbers of slaves. Most white Southerners did not possess such servants. At first, few Scots and Scotch-Irish kept slaves. The Scotch-Irish had come to the country in part because of their own political and economic slavery. Persons of English extract owned more slaves than others.

Some Statistics

In 1859 farms in Prince William County would run from a few to 300-400 acres with a number of tracts around 150-200 acres. The value of the land in 1859 was $10-$12 per acre.

Gilbert Moxley owned 331 acres valued at $4,634.00 and taxed at $18.51 according to the Prince William County, Virginia Land Tax Books, 1782-1861.

There was considerable change in the population of Prince William County during the 19th century. After the original top soil was depleted, many farmers left and went west. On the other hand, Charles Green imported guano and salts to improve fertility.[2] Cotton and tobacco did not grow well in the area so there was less demand for black labor than in other areas of the South. A number of Quakers from New York and New Jersey purchased land in the county and discouraged slavery. For these reasons, many slaves were sold South.

In 1790 Virginia's black population was 43.4 percent of the total. In 1860 it was 43.3 percent. According to the Personal Property Tax Lists, Prince William County, Virginia, for the year 1860, in a section surveyed by R.F. Brawner around Greenwich, there were 762 free white males above the age of 16. There were 791 slaves who have attained the age of 16. In addition, there were 619 white males exempted because of bodily infirmities, 46 free male Negroes and 874 slaves who had attained the age of 12.

Most of the residents of the area either had no slaves or only one or two. (The following persons are buried in Greenwich Cemetery.) Personal Property Tax lists for the same period indicate that Joseph Cockerille had 4 adult slaves; Thomas W. Edmonds 2 adult and 2 who had attained the age of 12; J. W. Fitzhugh 1-3; Howson Hooe 0-0; Michael House 2-2; Eliza Green Low 2-1; Andrew Low 0-0; William L. McIntosh 0-0 and James H. Moore 2-2.

Englishman, Charles Green, owned slaves. The 1840 Savannah census revealed that he had two male and one female slaves living in his household on what is now Oglethorpe Avenue.[3] In 1860 he also had 7 adult slaves and 9 who had not reached the age of 13 at Greenwich where he had a second residence and sheepfarm. One of these was Brooks a black coachman.[4]

The Reverend Thomas Bloomer Balch, Presbyterian Minister who lived in the area, owned slaves, some 9 persons in 1860. He married Susan Carter of the wealthy and distinguished Virginia family in Fairfax. Possibly Susan inherited the slaves from her father.

Joseph Arthur Jeffries of Fauquier County on occasion visited the parson. He said of Balch,

"From being a man of considerable means, he was literally eaten out by a number of Negro

64

slaves that he owned and kept around him, for the most part in idleness, while his wife and children did most of the necessary domestic work. It is said to be fact that in winter one of his Negro men would go to him and say, "Master, it is snowing hard and there is not wood at the woodpile, what must we do?" He would reply, "You had all better go to bed and cover up warm till the storm is over."[5]

In some areas, slaveholders treated their slaves brutally, justifying their treatment because they considered slaves to be only property. On the other hand, Southerners like Balch treated slaves with care and affection and as members of their household. The same endearment seemed to exist in the household of Charles Green. Brooks, the black coachman, drove Mrs. Lucy Green, to Macon, Georgia to confer with her husband. Their son, Edward Green, "misses Brooks particularly: so does his brother Gilbert."[6] While slaves and masters often had close relationships at work and even in the home; socially the lines of separation were sharp.

An Interesting Contrast

Slaves sometimes participated in the worship of white churches. Greenwich and Warrenton Presbyterian and other sanctuaries had slave galleries. Generally, in churches in the area, blacks were not only segregated in the balcony but denied vote and office. Many did receive the Sacrament of the Lord's Supper. After the Civil War, joint worship ceased for the most part.

Warrenton and Greenwich Presbyterian Churches were tied together with one minister and a common Session for several years. The minutes reveal that prior to the Civil War Warrenton had four slaves as members, Greenwich none.

It is possible that some blacks may be buried in the Greenwich Church Cemetery, but there are no records that this is true. As a child, Mrs. Minnie McMichael, member of Greenwich

Church, remembers a service for one black person being buried on the property which now belongs to her son, Earle. Sunken ground and depressions indicate a number of graves. No markers are visible. The property was earlier known as Weaver's Plantation.[7]

St. Paul's Episcopal Church of nearby Haymarket still has cemetery by-laws which specifically exclude persons of African descent from being buried there. At Leesburg Presbyterian, deceased black members were buried in graves alongside white members with whom they had not been permitted to sit inside the building, "an interesting contrast between time and eternity."

Slave owners instructed blacks in the Bible. Some promoted conversion among the slaves. Others were afraid that the implication of "one in Christ" would endanger black servility.

While slave owners taught a basic morality to slaves, little effort was given to controlling sexual affairs since reproduction was profitable to the owners. Charles Green seemed to have exerted more than usual concern. Anne Green said of the Green slaves that "their matrimonial affairs became so tangled during the war that a parson rode to The Lawn each Christmas to marry all couples afresh to the consorts of the moment. It was more respectable."[8]

Criminal Intercourse

The minutes of the Greenwich Session meeting of June 10, 1860 reveal that

> The Moderator, Rev. J. W. Pugh, called the elders to deal with a "common rumor, that Anne, a servant of Mr. P. S. Johnson and a member of this church, has had a child born to her, she being unmarried and further that said Anne has been guilty of further conduct unbecoming a Christian in falsely accusing a member of the Church of seeking to have criminal intercourse with her."[9]

On June 23rd, Anne appeared before the Session to answer charges of fornication and falsehood against her. Anne admitted to the birth of the child, but said that she did not think she was committing a sin since she planned to marry the father. Her marriage to him was prevented by the father being sold by his owner, Mr. Tavenner.

Two other slave women were brought to testify that Anne has said in their presence that Mr. Johnson had "twice endeavored to have criminal intercourse with her and wanted to keep her as his mistress." The Session found Anne guilty of both charges of fornication and falsehood and expelled her from the Warrenton church.

Masters were especially concerned about the use of alcohol by blacks. A white member of the Greenwich Church, Charles Kulp, appeared before the Session to answer charges of breaking the Sabbath, card playing and the "constant practice of selling liquor to slaves and all others who wanted to purchase."[10] Charles Green was appointed his counsel for defense, but Kulp was suspended until he showed satisfactory signs of repentance, which he never did.

A Guilty Conscience

Southern Christians lived in a secular culture which pressured them to behave in manners which their Christian convictions told them were sinful. This produced considerable internal conflict. Some historians say this underlying sense of guilt may have been a major contribution to the loss of the Civil War by the South.

The slavery issue and the Civil War still influence the theology of the South. Many Southerners adopted a "purity of the church" attitude which maintained that the church should remain separate and apart from all social action. Piety was relegated to no profanity, fornication or alcohol. The religious emphasis was on personal salvation as opposed to political involvement. A "purity of the church" concept seems strange since prior to the end of the war, the church was one of the greatest influences in Southern society and had much to do with the support of the war effort. Ministers exerted much influence and regularly preached on social and political issues, including protests against abolition.

Send Them to Liberia

Virginia came close to passing a bill for the abolition of slavery in 1832, but the issue was lost in the House of Delegates by 7 votes. Robert E. Lee favored gradual emancipation. Members of the African Colonization Society sought emancipation and removal to Africa with financial compensation to owners. President Monroe had earlier worked out such agreements with Liberia. Rev. Thomas Bloomer Blach took a great deal of interest in Liberia. He was an active member of the Colonization Society and apparently an agent for it.[11] He favored sending slaves to Liberia before the war changed the political issues. The "Savannah Daily Morning News," June 13, 1853 said, "The American Colonization Society and its auxiliaries have sent out to Liberia, since 1832, in their various expeditions 7,457 persons." "The Savannah Daily Morning News" of June 16, 1853 reveals that the treasurer of the Georgia Colonization Society was Charles Green.[12]

Free At Last

Lincoln finally delivered his Emancipation Proclamation. In 1863 Charles Green's slaves discovered they were free, and they "departed capering one morning to return the same night it having occurred to them that there's no place like home when nothing else offers."[13]

Freedom for slaves meant massive adjustments for the war-torn South. Virginia did not suffer as did South Carolina in the Reconstruction era. But it was difficult for persons of Prince William County to get used to the change in the status of the Afro-American. Michael House, Elder in Greenwich Church, sent a letter to his brother, John House, of Morresville, Indiana, dated

January 11, 1868. Revealing typical feelings of white superority and prejudice, commonly acceptable in his day, he wrote

They have the elective franchise and was compelled to vote the radical tickets for delegates to a convention to frame a constitution for our state to suit the radical congress. The negroes were formed in what they call a union league and under that league they are sworn to support that party and many of them would have voted the conservative ticket but were afraid to do so. In fact many did and were immediately lynched and many were scared on the penalty of death. Now just think here are these poor ignorant people just from bondage who have but very little knowledge of our political matters who as the President says (truly too) does not know how to cast a vote and in fact many had forgot what names they registered under and on that account could not vote. And here these votes are forced on us to form a convention to make our state convention when I think the very best of our men should only have voted. I am opposed to universal suffrage to the white people. I would not be opposed to the negro voting if he were capable and in time when they become more enlightened than it will be time enough. But most assuredly they were better off in slavery than now. Of course there are some exceptions. But as a whole they were better off. We see nothing here what it is further south but it is enough seen here to confirm what I have said. They are lounging around many half clad and not enough to eat. They could get plenty of work to do if they would but won't until necessity compels them and as a matter of course that makes them dishonest and many have flattered themselves that

69

they would get farms by confiscation but if ever that comes to pass there will be a war of races. Now as for myself I care nothing about slavery, but I feel for them who had scarcely any other property and Lincoln had no more authority (than I had) under the constitution of the United States to set them at liberty. He said it was a military necessity, but now that is stopped."[14]

The South did not have the will to win the war. The North proved not to have the will to pursue victory in the Reconstruction. Many Southerns were in one way relieved not to have to support slaves they did not need or their consciences disapproved, but they had no intention of giving up control over blacks. The war may have been lost over slavery and independence, but the peace was "won--for state rights, white supremacy, and honor. In this way, the South could claim 'a moral if not a military, victory.'"[15]

The Settlement

After the war, free blacks were often employed as servants in Greenwich community. There seems to have been little tenant farming as occurred in other parts of the South. Many Negroes moved looking for better opportunities.

Some of the blacks in the area settled in a nearby area known as "the settlement" shown on the Fauquier county map as Greenville. Robert Turner, 83 years old, when interviewed in 1991, said that after the Civil War, his ancestor, Silas Green, who had been a slave was given 10 or 11 acres. Silas Green built a little log house, the first in the community, and it was for this Green that the community was named.

Robert Turner does not know who gave his ancestor the land. It is possible that there was some connection between Silas Green and Charles Green of Greenwich since slaves were sometimes named for their masters. Charles Green may have provided the land for Silas Green.

Turner worked in the kitchen at The Lawn, the Green residence, for the family of Ann Green Mackall when he was a little boy, he said. His job was to help with the pots and pans and tend to the fire. He later worked across the road for the family of Mary Green Veeder.

Greenville community once had a store and a public grammar school. It still has a church, Little Zion Baptist, which was organized in 1879 with the help of the Greenwich Oakdale Baptist minister, Rev. Burr Dulin. The first place of worship was a brush arbor with four poles, and services could be conducted only in good weather, said Robert Turner.[16]

Before he died, Oakley Taylor of Greenwich told James Cooke that The Reverend Alexander Broadnax Carrington, minister at Greenwich Presbyterian Church, and who remained in the community until he died in 1910, would ask to be driven over to Greenville to perform wedding ceremonies when there was no pastor at Little Zion Baptist Church.[17]

In her will of October 31, 1906, Charles Green's third wife, Aminta Elizabeth Green, said that since their son, Andrew Low Green, had died, the portion of the estate that had been determined for him should go, "as a modest memorial to my husband, to The Georgia Infirmary of Savannah, Georgia." Green was greatly interested in the work there. It "is believed to be the oldest institution in this country for relief and protection of aged and afflicted Negroes." As a result, a number of "Uncle" Lias's may have received some comfort in their last years.[18]

CHAPTER NINE
THE ECCENTRIC CLERGYMAN

Thomas Balch was an unusual clergyman of the 1800's, and some may have thought him eccentric. Still, he possessed a remarkable mind and a simple piety. He made a personal impact on Northern Virginia during his day.

Famous Father

Rev. Stephen Bloomer Balch, the father of Thomas, was born April 5, 1747 on Deer Creek, Harford County, Maryland. He graduated at Princeton College in 1774. He was a captain in the Calvert County Militia during the Revolution and aided in repulsing the British on the Patuxent River and Chesapeake Bay.

Stephen Balch accepted a call to found a Presbyterian church in Georgetown, D. C. He began work on March 16, 1780 and remained there until his death 53 years later. Among his friends were George Washington and Thomas Jefferson. Stephen married Elizabeth Beall.[1]

Reverend Hezekiah I. Balch, uncle of Thomas, was the first signer of the Mecklenburg (North Carolina) Declaration of Independence in May, 1775.

Prankish Young Man

Thomas Bloomer Balch was born February 28, 1773 in Georgetown. Since his prominent father's church was near the Capital, he got to know a number of famous politicians. Stephen required the young Thomas to sit next to the pulpit in order to keep him quiet during church services. One Sunday when the prayer was extremely long, Thomas lost his patience. He reached over, got his father's spectacles off the pulpit, put them on, opened the hymn-book and said, "Come, my brethren, while the pra`r is going on, let us sing a hime."

One day when his father was absent from home, several couples came by the house to be married. Thomas, a little older at this time, decided to perform the ceremony. "So, in prankish feat, without ban or surplice, [he] went through a form of marriage, the parties being none the wiser, and it is hoped, none the less happy, for being married by the son instead of the father."[2]

Learned Fellow

Stephen Balch provided a good education for his son. Thomas took to learning readily. He enjoyed reading and did well in school. He graduated from the College of New Jersey in 1813 and Princeton Theological Seminary 1817 (Hampden-Sydney College conferred an honorary DD on him in 1860). Daniel Webster is supposed to have described him as the most learned man he had ever known.[3] Julia Balch, his daughter, said he studied classic lore and entered realms of thought others hadn't considered.

Thomas read good literature and soon began writing. He also loved nature. In 1849 he related a summer experience west of the Blue Ridge at Forest Inn near a stream by the name of Mossy Creek. "Woman had not then so spread out her charms as to entangle him in the sundry perplexities of life." He devoted the summer to studying and enjoying the geography.[4]

Unsettled Parson

Baltimore Presbytery ordained Thomas on October 31, 1816. For several years he assisted his father in the church at Georgetown. He accepted a call to Snow Hill, Rehoboth and Pitts Creek, Maryland on July 19, 1820. Snow Hill is the oldest Presbyterian Church in America.

Thomas Balch was never settled as a pastor after he left Maryland. He is listed as a missionary in Fairfax County from 1829-36. His brother-in-law, Septimus Tuston, had been a regular preacher at Greenwich, Virginia between 1825 and 1842. This connection may have led to Thomas becoming the stated supply at Warrenton and Greenwich between 1836-38 and again from 1874-78. He also supplied at Prince William and Nokesville.[5]

Ringwood

Just after he accepted the call to the churches in Maryland, Thomas Balch married Susan Carter of Fairfax, Virginia. Susan was the daughter of Charles Beale Carter of Shirley. Charles Beale Carter was an uncle of General Robert E. Lee. No doubt the marriage into the prominent and wealthy family helped Thomas financially.

When Thomas and Susan moved to Prince William and Fauquier Counties, they bought a place between Auburn and Greenwich on State Highway 603 near its intersection with State Highway 669. He called the property Ringwood. Part of the structure was later remodeled and remains today.[6]

Thomas Balch bought another piece of property at what is now 10214 Lonesome Road, closer to Nokesville. He deeded the property to his son, Chalmas Page, September 10, 1869. He had to go to court October 12, 1875 because the title was contested. In October 1878 the land was sold to Julia R. Balch. She did not keep it long.[7] Charles Roberston, who later lived in the house, said that when he and his brother would misbehave, his mother would tell them, "Old Chalmas Balch will come back and get you." James Cooke of Greenwich said he spent time there as a boy and remembers the story.

Helpmate

Ringwood or Macomb Manse, as it was sometimes called, appears to have been a happy place. Daughter, Julia thought of the home as a "loved retreat."[8] Julia remembered her mother, Susan, as one who experienced joys, disappointments, cares, tears, sunlight, "but shadows few." She saw her mother as an accomplished person who possessed rare gifts and culture.

Apparently Susan was an enthusiastic Christian. As a young woman, she left tracts by the way-side between Salona and Georgetown. Her stepfather came by shortly on horseback and gathered these leaflets. He took them to his daughter, not realizing that she was the one who had placed them along the road.[9]

Takes Queer Texts

Thomas had the enviable position of being financially secure enough to do some church work, relate closely to a large family, do a little farming, keep up with politics, and feel confident in high ranking social connections. He spent a lot of time reading and writing. The library at Ringwood was so small, that he had to depend a good deal on his neighbors for mental entertainment.

Joseph Arthur Jeffries of Fauquier County said as a child he visited the Balch home and found

> Dr. B. was simple, unpretentious and most affectionate, as well as one of the drollest of men in his attire. I have heard that he used to say that he feared that tidiness was his besetting sin. When he wore shoes at all at his home they were down at heel. When visiting his house as a child I usually found him without coat, vest, collar or cravat, slip shod with a domestic flannel shirt on, and knit yarn suspenders supporting his trousers. The old gentleman never waxed fat, but I saw him kick once when a Warrenton drug clerk in his proprietor's absence applied to the old man's back a strengthening plaster so hot that the substance on it was running. So confiding was he, that this young man was able to mollify and persuade him that the pastor was in the very best condition to relieve his trouble."[10]

Julia said he had "left the applause of the world behind."[11] Thomas often read Psalm 23. When he had afternoon and evening devotions he kneeled for prayer. His detachment from world affairs and piety gave him peace of mind.

Thomas was considered a good pulpiteer. Julia said he "preached a saviour crucified." Jeffries said he was "apt to take queer texts in preaching, but not from affectation. I heard him once preach from 'He is the rose of Sharon and the lily of the Valley' and again from 'Jerushen waxed fat and kicked.'"[12]

Thomas Bloomer Balch probably in some ways leaned towards the Old School Theology of the Presbyterians of his day. It was more traditional and perhaps more legalistic. The New School tended to be more fervent and more evangelistic, and this group of Presbyterians was abolitionistic. Balch must have found himself caught between the two extremes, especially as the Civil War began. Serious concerns developed in the church courts.

Church Courts

Just after the Civil War started, Potomac Presbytery, meeting at Greenwich at its last meeting until the end of the war, considered a motion to renounce the jurisdiction of the General Assembly and move towards forming a Southern General Assembly. Balch asked to be excused from voting. The request was granted. The resolution was adopted unanimously. Apparently Balch found himself in a personal conflict, as many others did, concerning secession and the role and place of the church in it.[13] Presbytery didn't meet again until September 15, 1865, again at Greenwich. Balch is not recorded as being present on this occasion.

Balch may not have attended because of confusion about the legality of the Presbytery. The churches of Potomac Presbytery that had stayed in the Union in the D. C. - Maryland area claimed to be the true Presbytery. They kept the name of the Presbytery and the minutes. The group of Southerners changed their name to Rappahannock Presbytery.

However, Thomas Blach soon took part in Presbytery on a regular basis. He was directed to prepare a memorial for a deceased minister, Rev. Elias Harrison. He failed to be present or to send in the memorial at the appointed time. Another minister was given the task. He was "excused for his non-compliance with order of Presbytery" October 5, 1866. Thomas showed up at a later meeting, June 1867, and read his memorial. Presbytery elected him as a commissioner to the General Assembly meeting in Nashville, Tennessee, October 18, 1867.

In June 1867, Presbytery placed Balch on a special committee of Presbytery to consider the duty of the denomination to the "freed people within our bounds, and the best mode of discharging it."[14] Balch seemed to have a real concern for the blacks, though neither the Presbytery nor the denomination ever did much in this area of ministry.

Highly Regarded

Thomas and Susan Balch's last years may have been difficult. The Civil War and its aftermath may have put them in a financial strain. In a letter, December 19, 1871, Charles Green asked Dr. Moxley to

> make another of the miryest rides in all the country-side, to poor Mr. Balch, having first satisfied your purse with $25 which I desire you to present him wishing my kindest regards. Pray do this before Christmas Day if you possibly can.[15]

In a letter to his good friend W.W. Corcoran, December 9, 1869, Thomas thanked him for his elegant Christmas present which made him weep. He also says, "Hope that an Indian summer will soon come, when I hope to get down for my eye is paining me."[16]

For a number of years, Balch was the oldest living Princeton alumnus. According to his memorial, April 1878, his strength had gradually declined for a long time. Fatal illness continued for about three weeks. "To the last he had a clear mind and he uttered many expressions of faith and hope up to his last breath."[17]

He died February 14, 1878. His wife, Susan, had expired the year before. His friend, W. W. Corcoran, provided tombstones for the couple, and they are buried in the Greenwich Presbyterian Cemetery underneath the large Holly tree. During his life time, Thomas Balch had "become almost as highly regarded by Virginia Presbyterians as his famous father had been by the citizens of Georgetown and Washington."[18]

Children[19]

1. Ann Carter Balch was born in 1821, in Fairfax County, Virginia. She married Mr. Ashton and had two children, Charles and Thomas, who lived in Fauquier County, Virginia. She died before her mother.

2. Elizabeth Balch was born about 1824 in Virginia. She married R. M. Carter, a planter in Alabama. They had three children: Fitzhugh, who was in the United States Army at Fort Henry, near Baltimore; Thomas, a lawyer at San Diego, and Cassius, who was in the United States mail service. Elizabeth died during the war, and the family didn't hear about her death for 7 months.

3. Robert Monroe Balch was born May 7, 1826, in Virginia. He moved to Haywood County, Tennessee. He was a large, fine looking man, with most courtly manners, and was Lieutenant Colonel in the Confederate Army under General N. B. Forrest. He was in the Western Army and at the fight at Fort Donelson and had his horse shot out from under him, but mounted another. After the war, he was a lawyer and cotton broker in Memphis. In 1871 he was killed in Crittendon County, Arkansas by squatters on lands there which were owned by him and his brother, Charles.

4. Charles Carter Balch was born in 1828 at Snow Hill, Maryland. He was a captain in the Confederate States Army and served under General Forrest. He fought at the Battle of Fort Donelson. He lived in Lansing, Arkansas.
5. Harriet Balch died young.
6. Chalmas Page Balch lived on the property on Lonesome Road. His occupation was farm laborer.
7. Linnaeus Balch died young.
8. William Cowper Balch was a private in the "Black Horse Troop," Company H. Fourth Virginia.
9. Felix Neff Balch was twin to William Cowper Balch.
10. Mary Landon Balch was born in Georgetown, D. C. She lived in Washington, was highly educated and conducted a school which made a specialty of preparing candidates for the Civil Service examinations. She died in 1899. Mary must have been called Mollie, Jeffries said.

Dr. B. devoted much personal attention to the education of his daughters. The presence of visitors while he was teaching did not seem to distract him at all from his work. He was devoted to his daughter, Miss Mollie, who is now a most successful educator in Washington, D. C. The story is told of him that someone, when she was very young, mentioned in his presence the prospect of her marrying and leaving him. He said, "What, my daughter Mollie! If any man came for her, I would take my horsewhip and whip him around the world." I never could get rid of the idea that Lore Lytton had his like in mind when he portrayed the character of Pisistra as Caxton's father. We do not find his kind with us any more.[20]

11. Julia Ringwood Balch was born in 1837. She conducted a school with her sister, Mary, in D. C. She died August 25, 1905. Julia, who seemed to possess the culture and refinement of her mother, loved the home place and was quite fond of Jane Alexander Milligan who ran Ringwood

Academy. She was probably the only one born at Ringwood Manse. The census of 1860 indicates that only Chalmas Page and William Cowper of the male children were in the area, Bristoe Station Post Office, at that time.[21]

The Session and Register Minutes of Warrenton and Greenwich Presbyterian Churches 1855-67 list only the names of Susan C. Balch and Ann Balch as members. Ann was dismissed in 1855 or 1856.[22]

Publications [23]

Balch authored several books and articles. He frequently wrote for *The Southern Literary Messenger and The Christian World*, and he published articles in *Christianity* and *Literature, 1826, The Office and Work of a Bishop, A Miniature Poem, "Our Town"* and *Reminiscences of Georgetown, D.C.*

CHAPTER TEN
A MAN OF MEANS

We Surrender

General William T. Sherman marched from Atlanta to the sea, burning and pillaging as he went. Savannah awaited Tecumseh with some hope of rescue but little confidence that the Yankee general could be kept away. Staring at defeat, defending General William J. Hardee evacuated his men to safety to South Carolina before any serious fighting took place. On December 21, 1864, Mayor Richard Arnold and his aldermen rode out the Augusta Road to surrender the city. With this party went Mr. Charles Green, Englishman and wealthy merchant. Sherman was absent at the time so the Georgians met General Oliver O. Howard or General John W. Geary. They handed over the proud city to the Yankees at 4:30 in the morning. When official courtesies had been exchanged, Green went forward and said to Howard, "General, we surrender the city only upon one condition."

With some scorn Howard replied, "Sir, a conquered city has not the privilege of making terms of surrender."

"Nonetheless," responded Mr. Green, "I insist upon the acceptance of one condition before capitulation, namely that General Sherman and his staff make use of my house for headquarters during their stay in Savannah."

Later Green approached General Sherman as he rode to the Pulaski Hotel where he expected to stay. He offered Sherman his home for headquarters. "If you don't take it," he said, "some other general will. I much prefer you."[1] Some have wondered why Green made the offer.

Charles Green came to Savannah from Liverpool England in 1833 to seek his fortune. He found it in exporting cotton. He proved to be a good businessman and soon amassed considerable wealth. In all, Charles Green, Sr. had three wives: "And it was said, 'First he burroughed,' married Catharine Burroughs, 'Second he hunted,' married Lucy Hunton, and 'Third he fished,' married Aminta Elizabeth Fisher."[2] His first wife, Catherine Jane Burrough, whom he had married in 1837, died in 1842.[3]

In 1850 Green married Lucinda Ireland Hunton of Prince William County, Virginia. The same year he began construction in Savannah of a house at a cost of £50,000. He put the property in Lucy's name along with an additional $30,000 which was invested in stocks for her.

The house is a striking blend of Georgian and Victorian Gothic with battlements, stained-glass windows and rooms filled with Italian sculpture and European paintings. The graceful curved stairway with skylight above is a feature common in other houses designed by the architect, John S. Norris of New York. The dome has vents and gas fixtures which when lighted created an updraft, thus a unique form of ventilation for the house on hot summer days. It also contained a cistern on the roof for a bath, or at least tanks for baths, which may have been supplied with water by servants. The house has covered porches on three sides. His home, now known as the Green-Meldrim House, is a National Historical Landmark and also the Parish House of St. John's Episcopal Church.

Into this residence Green brought General Sherman. He escorted him to the second floor and turned over his own suite to him. He, his wife Lucy and children Gilbert, Edward, Douglas, Anne, Lucy and Mary had to find accommodations elsewhere, perhaps some of them in the servants quarters which was located behind the house. This latter building is now the rectory for St. John's. It's possible that Green had sent his family to his summer home in Greenwich, Virginia. At any rate, they were used to their father's penchant for entertaining generals and other dignitaries whenever he could.

Charles Green was a man who enjoyed social occasions so was pleased when Sherman invited him to a dinner party of twenty in Green's home on Christmas Day. Green offered his silver and china for the occasion, as well as his house. The guests may have laughed over a story that an Episcopal bishop had asked Sherman's consent to pray for the Rebel cause. "Hell, yes," the general had said, "Jeff Davis and the Confederate government need all the prayer they can get."

A Busy General

For the most part Sherman was a busy Federal officer, and his guests or visitors had to do with military affairs. U. S. Treasury agent, A. G. Browne, tried to claim all the captured cotton for his department. Sherman refused. Browne later suggested that Sherman send a wire to President Lincoln, which he did from Green's house. "I beg to present you as a Christmas gift, the City of Savannah, with one hundred and fifty heavy guns, and plenty of ammunition, also twenty-five thousand bales of cotton."

Lincoln read the telegraph on Christmas Eve. Newspapers picked it up, and the official announcement created a sensation in the North. Looking for a hero, the Northern public found one in Sherman. Browne became his friend for life.

Secretary of War, Edwin M. Stanton, arrived in Savannah and pressed Sherman concerning his troops' practice towards Negroes. When the Secretary persisted in exploring racial problems, Sherman invited twenty blacks - most of them preachers - to Green's house. Possibly for the first time, blacks took part in a political caucus. Attempts were made to better understand the position of the freed slaves and to begin plans to improve their plight.

A Thousand Pins

When a Miss Moodie visited Green, the Englishman asked her if she wished to be introduced to Sherman. "Not for the world." Green took her upstairs to look at a painting and pointed out that General Sherman's apartments were next door. She wrinkled her nose with disdain.

"Don't you want him to rest comfortably?"

"Indeed not! I wish a thousand papers of pins were stuck in that bed and that he was strapped down to them," with an expression indicating wonder as to how a good Southerner could have *him* in his home.[4]

Two reasons have been offered as to Green's hospitality. One, that by offering his home he spared some citizen of the Confederate States the "ignominy of having his house requisitioned by Sherman." Green said jestingly that it was as much from a desire to preserve his property against the "vandal hands of a victorious soldiery." At any rate, he helped soften Sherman's attitude towards the city.

While Green may have been hurt some socially for his relationship with Sherman, he did not suffer financially. By 1868 business was again booming in Savannah. Green prospered, and his company stayed very busy.

Years later Sherman revisited Green at his Savannah home. Together they remembered the "good old days." Perhaps Green's reason for opening his doors to Sherman was quite simple: He liked prominent and interesting company. Anyway, while they were not always good, Yankees couldn't be all bad.

CHAPTER ELEVEN
THE BELOVED TEACHER

A tablet on the sanctuary wall of the Greenwich Presbyterian Church honors Jane Alexander Milligan as the founder of Ringwood Female Seminary. It reads, "For nearly thirty years a devout member of this church, she served her Master faithfully." The tablet was dedicated by her old scholars and friends in "loving remembrance."

The educator, who was born in Georgetown in 1827, began teaching at the early age of 15. She probably started Ringwood Female Seminary with the encouragement of Rev. Thomas Bloomer Balch about 1852, assuming she began about the time she joined Greenwich Presbyterian Church. Balch, a learned Presbyterian minister, on occasion had been the minister at Greenwich. The Seminary was located at his home, Ringwood Manse. It appears that he added one or two wings to his house for this purpose. Part of the building survives and has been remodeled. It stands back from the highway near the intersection of Rogues Road (State Route 602) and Ringwood Road (State Route 669).

Public school education was not satisfactory in the 1800's, particularly for those who intended to go to college and those who wanted more Christian and cultural influence in their learning. Miss Milligan's school was a boon for local families. The school was for girls, some of which came from a distance. Some men attended as day students, said Agnes Wood Godfrey, now of Baltimore, who remembers family members talking about the school.[1]

One local person, Mrs. Mae Ellis, the oldest member of Greenwich Presbyterian Church, has a medal given to her mother when she was a student at Ringwood Female Seminary. The gold keepsake reads, "Miss Milligan - 1880 - F. S. Moore. Excellence in scholarship."

In a poem, Julia Ringwood Balch, who had been a pupil of Miss Alexander, paid tribute to her talent and her judicious skill which made learning a "loved employ." The fair lady was "loved by all." She trained "both heart and mind."[2] The front piece of the poem has a pen sketch of the building. Julia Ringwood Balch and her sister, Mary L., daughters of Thomas Bloomer Balch, operated a private school in Washington, D. C. to prepare persons for civil service examinations.

In 1936 Louise Lewis of Rectortown, Virginia, interviewed Kate Nickens who had lived on the place. She said that Miss Milligan conducted a select girls boarding school of about 14 scholars. The girls were required to attend church at Greenwich Presbyterian, and Miss Janie would take them there herself in an ox cart. According to Aunt Kate, the girls went singing most of the time.[3]

The Nickens family purchased the property sometime after the school was closed. The family of the late James Mac Nickens and Kate Chambers Nickens possesses a photograph of the building taken about 1900.[4] Members of the family recall when as children playing at the house, that they saw an old trunk full of letters and papers, some of which dated back into the 1700's. The trunk was stolen during a time the house was not occupied.

At one time Miss Alexander moved the Seminary to Greenwich. According to Mrs. Mae Ellis the school was conducted at the Veeder house on the corner of Burwell (State Road 604) and Vint Hill (State Road 215). After a time Miss Alexander returned the school to Ringwood where it remained until 1877 when she died.

Miss Milligan had requested that she be buried under an old tree on the place, a spot she often went to read. Instead she was interred at Oak Hill Cemetery in Georgetown. Burial records reveal she succumbed to apoplexy. The tombstone reads, "Our beloved sister, Jane Alexander Milligan, Born January 16, 1827. Died July 13, 1882."[5]

CHAPTER TWELVE
THE WICKED STOREKEEPER

On August 3, 1856 at Greenwich, the Session met at the call of the moderator, Rev. John W. Pugh, to inquire into rumors about the character of brother Mahlon Kulp.[1] Some persons said that since Brother Kulp's connection with the Church he had been guilty of playing cards for money and doing this on the Sabbath day.

Brother Kulp, the accused, was present and waived the regular constitutional notice. He requested immediate trial. Messrs. W. T. Hall and James Riley testified against him. The accused gave his testimony and then withdrew from the Session. After full consultation and deliberation, the Session unanimously agreed that the credibility of the witnesses was unimpeached and that Brother Mahlon Kulp had been guilty of conduct unbecoming a Christian.

Because he had been engaged in the company of the "wicked irreligious" in the practice of card-playing for money, he had thus brought reproach upon the cause of Christ. The Session excluded Brother Kulp from church privileges until he should produce satisfactory evidence of his repentance. At such time, they said, they would restore him to membership.

The Moderator, Rev. J. W. Pugh, called a meeting of the Session at Greenwich on May 2, 1858 to inquire into certain rumors about Brother John Kulp, "Deacon in this Church." Some persons said that Brother Kulp had frequently sold liquor to slaves and whites on the Sabbath. They said he had been guilty of other conduct inconsistent with the character and profession of a follower of Christ Jesus. The Session voted to inform Mr. John Kulp of the rumors. They requested him to give an explanation or refutation of the said accusations in order to avoid their preferring formal charges.

On June 6 the Session met, and the moderator presented a letter from Mr. John Kulp. The letter was not deemed a satisfactory refutation of the rumors since Brother Kulp was charged by "Common Fame" with conduct unbecoming a professed follower of Jesus Christ. The Session cited him to appear before them at the hour of 9 AM on Sabbath, June 20 for the purpose of answering the said charge and, in addition, to the charges of "wilful and deliberate lying."

Brother John Kulp did not make the June 20 date. The Session issued a new citation for him to appear on Sabbath, July 4. Brother John Kulp did not appear again whereupon the Session adjudged him guilty of contumacy. Nevertheless, in order to give him a fair trial, the Session went on to hear his case anyway. The elders assigned Charles Green to manage the defense of the accused, and the Session heard the various testimonies.

Sabbath Breaker

Mr. James Moore declared that he "had frequently seen the accused selling liquor on Sabbath - that he (Kulp) received in his (Moore's) presence money in payment for said liquor." "Mr. Kulp was in the constant habit of selling liquor to slaves and all others who wanted to purchase. Did not stop for Sabbath more than any other day. Was in the habit of keeping open his store on Sabbath days until Church Time."

The Session gave consideration to Mr. Kulp's letter presented at the June 6 meeting. The counsel for defense, Charles Green, objected to its reception because the handwriting was not proven to be that of Mr. John Kulp. After consideration, "The Session concluded to lay aside the letter and abandon the specification of *wilful lying*" inasmuch as they deemed the other specification sufficient to establish inconsistent and censurable conduct.

After due deliberation, the Session declared that Brother John Kulp should be suspended from all Church privileges including Communion until he should give satisfactory evidence of his repentance.

During the Civil War, Session records were not well kept, but a summary statement shows that John Kulp and Mahlon Kulp were dismissed at their request.[2]

On Sept. 8, 1859, Presbytery approved the Session Records except for its holding a Judicial meeting on the Sabbath Day!

CHAPTER THIRTEEN
THE POOR PREACHER

One of the early ministers at Greenwich had a dispute with the church. The Reverend Robert Baker White was pastor from April 21, 1869 to November 22, 1877. Mr. White was born in Winchester, Virginia, March 10, 1816, the son of Judge Robert White. His grandfather, Robert White, was also a judge. Robert was educated at Hampden-Sydney College and Union Theological Seminary. He served churches in this area and in Tuscaloosa, Alabama where he resided during the Civil War.

Mr. White was the first regularly installed pastor the church had. It was just after the War Between the States, and hard times had hit the area. A spiritual and social breakdown had occurred. The countryside was stripped from the criss-crossing of armies. The slaves had been freed. A number of families had moved away during and after the hostilities. Money was scarce.

Tenuous Ties

At an adjourned meeting in Alexandria, November 9, 1877, Chesapeake Presbytery heard Rev. R. B. White and Elder Moxley "in reference to the condition of the church at Greenwich."[1] Perhaps life in the Greenwich Church had declined during this time period so that the pastor and church members were concerned about its existence. Likely, the connection between pastor and the members was critical. If a number were not attending, the church's future hung precariously. This would be disastrous because there had been only 33 or so on the roll when it went on a self-sustaining basis.

The next day, Saturday, shortly after Presbytery opened with prayer, Rev. R. B. White "asked leave of Presbytery to resign the pastoral charge" of the church. But before permission was granted Presbytery cited the church "to appear at Culpeper,

Virginia, November 22 at 12 PM and show cause if any why he should not be allowed to resign."

Presbytery appointed ministers, A. L. McMurrain and J. S. Scott and Elder N. R. Green, a "committee to visit Greenwich Church and effect - if possible - a pecuniary settlement between Pastor and people." The committee reported at the next meeting at Culpeper, November 22, 1877 and said they had met with elders Moxley, Fitzhugh and Catlett. They reported they heard statements from the minister and the committee.

It appeared to the committee that since Mr. White had a call and was installed, and that the amount of his salary was stated in the call, the obligation remained in force as long as he was the pastor of the church. The agreement remained binding until September 20, 1877. They said that Elder Moxley acknowledged that $130 was still due Dr. White.

Dr. White's call also stipulated that he would receive "payment of board," though the rate of payment or just what this consisted of was not specified.

Compromise

The committee admitted to Dr. White that he had a right to the $130 and the board that had been promised, "Yet while these are the facts in the case," there probably had been some misunderstanding on the part of the elders as to the binding nature of a call." In the interest of peace, they encouraged a compromise. So Greenwich and Dr. White agreed to part with the elders raising $130 during the coming 12 months and Dr. White giving up any claim due him in board. Presbytery approved the report. Rev. J. A. Scott was appointed to preach at Greenwich and declare the pulpit vacant. The minutes of the meeting noted that "Greenwich Church failed to appear in answer to citation" to be present.

Dr. White continued to live at Greenwich and was at that time about 62. His wife, Nannie Conway Blackwell, died in 1875. Dr. White parted this life at Greenwich, September 26, 1894. He became feeble minded. He fell out of an upstairs window at the old

Blackwell house and broke his neck in the flower bed.[2] In the minutes of the Synod of Virginia, October 1893, a memorial says,

> And Dr. White, although his last hours were clouded by the difficult breathing and the collapse of pneumonia that is produced by the shock of an accidental fall, which was the cause of his death, yet rallied sufficiently to express the firmest trust in the kind Heavenly Father, and the most loving reliance upon the gracious Saviour. Hence in leaving him with his God we mourn as those who have both hope and consolation.[3]

Final Indignity

White suffered a further affront. In the local church history, he is noted as Albert B. White instead of Robert B. White. Possibly this occurred because in a Synod publication his name appears beneath that of Albert B. Carrington. Because he was wrongly designated in the church history, his name is also incorrect on the recent plaque of ministers on the wall of the sanctuary of Greenwich Presbyterian Church.

The White's had at least one son, William Donaghe, born in 1851 in Alabama. He began teaching at Greenwich School in 1871 and continued until 1878. He then went to the University of Virginia and Union Theological Seminary and was a candidate for the ministry at Greenwich Presbyterian Church. He was ordained in 1882 and served some churches in the area. The record shows that between 1880-1890 he was "weak and infirm" and at Staunton (asylum). He later lived in D.C. and Arlington but died September 9, 1926 at Staunton, "thus closing a tragic life."

CHAPTER FOURTEEN
AN OLD TIMER

John Royall Cooke was born 5 years after the Civil War. He was tall and slender, raw boned with an athletic build. He had a long, thin face with an aquiline nose that had been broken playing football. Attractive and dignified, he was reserved, quiet, serious and sometimes stern. He did not joke a lot. He had some dry humor, but if he told a tale he "didn't let down much." Still he "talked to and knew everybody." He was friendly with most persons he contacted.

Ephraim

Cooke grew up about 30 miles from Greenwich. On a high bluff about 200 hundred yards from the Rappahannock River lie thick foundation walls, the only remains of his home, Mt. Ephraim, which burned in the 1980's. Ephraim, a Biblical word, means "that brings fruit or grows." Around 1800 at this site of great beauty, George Keith Taylor and his wife, Jane, built their house.[1] Jane was the youngest sister of Chief Justice John Marshall.

A daughter of this union, Anna Keith, married the Reverend J. J. Royall. He started Grove Presbyterian Church nearby what is now Goldvein and was pastor there for 16 years. He built "The Manse" one mile north of Mt. Ephraim, the land coming from Jane Marshall Taylor. Earlier the couple lived at Mt. Ephraim.[2] While walking to church on an icy Sunday morning just after crossing Big Branch, he dropped dead of apoplexy. It was 1856 and he was 50.

The main part of the Mt. Ephraim house was a two story light brick structure with porches on the front and back. J. J. Royall added a wooden section to the dwelling, probably around 1836. During the Civil War, the Federals set this part on fire. The three ladies in the house saved the brick section by hanging wet blankets against the door. Charred wood on the door continued to show up into the mid 1900's. The Royalls restored the house at the end of the war.[3]

Helen Matilda Royall, daughter of J. J. and Anna, married John Gordon Cooke, a medical doctor.[4] They had three sons and one daughter. One of the boys was John Royall Cooke, born on January 15, 1870. His father was 46 and his mother 28, John had a daughter, Sally, by his first marriage.

J. R. Cooke loved his home. As a boy, he played in the yard, "prospected" for gold,[5] hunted in the fields, walked along the Rappanhannock Canal[6] and fished in the river which can be seen and heard from the house site. He retained a fondness for the out-of-doors.

The family were members of the Grove Presbyterian Church where Grandfather Royall had been pastor. In 1976 Presbytery closed the church which was begun in 1835. Cooke's Calvanist heritage and a heavy dose of religion molded his character and personality. According to Mrs. N. K. Middlethon, sister of Royall and historian of the Grove Church in 1943, J. R. was the only minister from the congregation. He was "dedicated by his mother from earliest infancy to this sacred office." He was close to his mother until she died in 1900.[7]

A Good Student

After finishing studies locally, John Royal Cooke entered Central University in Richmond, Kentucky. The "Catalogue of Students" gave his residence as Pine View, Virginia.[8] He made the honor roll for 1989-90 in Greek, geology, German, Latin, logic, mathematics, physics and psychology. He received a BA Degree in 1891. A theological department was added that fall, and Cooke enrolled and studied there for the ministry. The department lasted only one year, but after another year's lapse it opened again in Louisville, said Dr. Al Winn former president of Louisville Seminary. Cooke got credit for being a member of the first class of Louisville Seminary.[9]

Cooke did not go to Louisville but went to Union seminary which at that time was at Hampden Sydney, Virginia. Cooke may have played football while at Central University. He told Raymond Spittle that he played at Hampden Sydney. He gave Raymond his football helmet which the family still possesses. Cook graduated from Union in 1894 and was ordained to preach by Transylvania Presbytery in 1895. He ministered in that area.[10]

How Much Can We Pay?

Cooke tranferred to Potomac Presbytery in which he became recognized as a "faithful and able presbyter." He began supplying Greenwich in 1906. The church sought him as their installed pastor earlier, but he did not agree to this permanent relationship for two more years. On August 22, the Session "ordered that a congregational meeting be held on 1st Sunday in September for the purpose of calling a pastor. Ordered that Deacons P. M. Boley, Jno House, and O. D. Ellis ascertain the sentiments of the congregation and the amount each member is willing to subscribe toward the support of a pastor." The salary was around $330 per year. The actual amount paid in 1909 was $216.

Agnes Elizabeth Wood Godfrey "can remember a big Santa sitting in a chair in the church. He was stuffed with sugar, oatmeal, cornmeal, flour, beans, rice etc. It was a gift to Rev. J. Royal Cooke. He didn't take any salary as it was Depression, 1930 or so. He didn't receive pay for more than one year during that period." On the other hand, Session records suggest he received more salary during the Depression than before or after. The minutes may have failed to note that it wasn't all paid or that Cooke asked to have his salary reduced.[11]

George M. Wood said that when he retired, the minister was making around $600 per year. The Rev. Mr. Cooke was not a man to worry about personal finances. The low salary that he had received did not appear to bother him. When it was time to call the next minister, some believed that Cooke may have influenced the congregation to keep the salary of the next pastor, Reverend T.K. Mowbray, low. There may have been some argument about the matter, and one of the elders seemed to be upset that Cooke was criticized. Wood said that he "missed what they were talking about which was that they were not speaking against Rev. Cooke but only saying the Rev. Cooke should have made us keep him in fair salary all along instead of giving it to us."

A Good Catch

The church furnished a manse. The first parsonage for a minister at Greenwich was erected at the persuasion of the third Mrs. Charles Green in 1906. The house was a substantial two story white frame building with spacious grounds. It had no indoor plumbing until the mid 1940's. The dwelling, located at 15012 Vint Hill Road, is no longer owned by the church.

Cooke moved into the new residence late in December of 1908. His study was on the premises. On March 23, 1909, the Session "approved the action of Elder Wood in buying a phone for the manse."

The 38 year old pastor was unmarried. A number of the single ladies found this a challenge, and some thought to catch him. But he was not interested, said Mae Ellis. His sister, Sally, who was 16 years older than the minister, came to help him keep house. She was a half sister, probably by her father's first marriage.

According to some reports, Sally, somewhat domineering, could unload on anyone who offended her. Raymond Spittle said Mr. Marshall who lived at the Washington or the old Moxley place nearby was something of a cantankerous bachelor. One night Marshall and Cooke engaged in a long chess game at the manse. Sally grew weary of company and told him to "go home and take the chess men with you." The Greenwich pastor hardly looked up when he said in his flat drawl. "Leave 'em lay where they are." And they did.

Sally died November 9, 1926 and is buried in the church cemetery. At her funeral, all the children from Greenwich School marched from the school house up to the church for the services, said June Spittle.

Sometime after Sally's death, Cooke's other sister, Nannie, Mrs. H. Keith Middlethon of Goldvein, moved in with him. She had also lived in Florida before her husband had died in 1920. Cooke referred to her as "Mrs. Middlethon" when speaking of her. Mrs. Middlethon was "sweet" especially in comparison with Sally.[12] She was an attractive person, "having been married may have mellowed her," one commented.[13] Mae Ellis said that Mrs. Middlethon's two sons, William Royall and Jonathan, lived with them at the manse. Cooke also boarded teachers from the school at the manse, said Newman Hopkins.

Somethimes He Mumbled

The preacher may not have been alone at home, but he was in the pulpit. He felt a responsibility for the morals of the community; at least this concern is remembered by the church members. Cooke would never marry anyone who had been divorced and sometimes preached against it. Sally, his sister, had been divorced, according to Marguerite Fountain. Some wondered at Sally's aplomb in the pew as her brother preached against the breaking up of a marriage from the pulpit.

Doris Beach said he once preached about couples living together without the benefit of matrimony, being concerned about that practice of some in the community. One woman retorted to another, "Well, he is living with a woman, and they're not married."

He also "took off on the trash that was in some of the popular magazines." He hit at "True Stories." He claimed it was a waste of time to read such things. Marguerite Fountain's mother laughed after such remarks, "Well I wonder if he has read some of these magazines since he knows so much about what is in them."

He got concerned about persons drinking too much and preached about that. Session records indicate that a couple of intemperate members in his earlier ministry at Greenwich were disciplined for the evil. Yet one remembers that Cooke said, "He liked the taste of alcohol and gasoline."

Cooke's reserved nature carried over into the pulpit. He tended to speak in a monotonous and deep tone. Sometimes his voice didn't register with the congregation, and it sounded like he was mumbling. Still, he could get "stirred up if something was going on in the community he didn't like. He'd let the congregation know about it, and then he raised his voice and almost hollered." He didn't often change his expression, said Reba Hopkins. On occasion while speaking, he moved down to the front level of the rostrum. In winter with the two potbelly stoves on each side giving off uneven heat, the congregation got pretty drowsy. A number went to sleep. Others waited him out, sometimes impatiently.

In 1909 he preached at Greenwich on the first Sunday of each month at the morning service; second Sunday, morning and night; third Sunday, night service; and fourth Sunday, morning service. The purpose of the staggered schedule was to permit Cooke's preaching at other points, including new church development. While at Greenwich, he helped begin and continued to serve at the Brentsville Presbyterian Church from 1910 - 1925. At times he was stated supply of Marshall and Delaplane (Westminister) Churches.

While Cooke seemed more moralistic than evangelistic, the church under him held annual revival services with a visiting preacher. He gave invitations to come forward. Selma Corder remembers accepting such an invitation, joining the church and being baptized. He appeared before the Session November 8, 1936.

He believed persons should "be worthy to receive communion, and that the Session should be strict in keeping a roll of communicants." But Cooke was not always as pious or strait laced as he appeared in the pulpit. Rev. Dr. Al Winn said that Lucy House told him that she and Mr. Cooke were in the church giving it a spring cleaning one day. Mrs. House and Mr. Cooke took the pipe of one of the two potbellied stoves down and a lot a black soot fell out all over the floor "Oh, the Devil," said the pastor.

"Why, Mr. Cooke!" exclaimed Lucy.

"Now, Lucy there's nothing in the Bible against taking the Devil's name in vain," replied J. Royall.

Treated Everybody the Same

Cooke usually met with the Youth. "He was always there to help us," said Minnie McMichael. He taught a few of them to play chess. Raymond Spittle said the only time he could recall him angry was when the Youth Group was meeting at the manse just after Pearl Harbor. When he learned of the attack, "Cooke raised and clinched his fist and with some umbrage he muttered, 'I'll just like to take them...'"

While he was friends with them, he believed "Young people should keep their mouths shut unless spoken to," said George M. Wood. On the other hand, Agnes Wood Godfrey remembered that at one of the youth meetings they played Tap Rabbit in which he also participated. She recalls that she went around the circle and tapped him. He then chased her and caught her, whereupon he was allowed the prize, to kiss the tapper.

He sometimes took the Youth to Mt. Ephraim for picnics and swimming in the Rappahannock. Cooke greatly strengthened the youth work and the Sunday School. Sometimes his brother, Keith, would come up from Goldvein and teach one of the classes.

Cooke took his pastoral duties seriously and seems to have visited on a regular basis. The pastor "treated everybody the same if they needed a minister." Marguerite Fountain remembers him coming by her house to speak with her of her plans for getting married. He suggested they go out in the garden to confer. The pre-marriage counseling was brief.

Agnes Godfrey said, "When I was married at the manse in 1936 by Mr. Cooke, Mrs. Middlethon said, 'Come into the dining room for it has been freshly painted." After the vows were spoken, my husband gave Mr. Cooke an envelope for the fee which contained about $2.00 in bills. Mr. Cooke gave me back the envelope and $2.00."[14]

Aggie said, "One day when Mr. Cooke came to call my sister went to the door. He asked, 'May I come in?' She replied, 'You can if your nose is clean.' Mother was horrified, but he enjoyed it like a kid."

Aggie's mother said, "Mr. Cooke was not too much younger than grandmother who was born in 1860. He was visiting in the home, and grandmother was serving coffee. She poured him a cup and later asked him if he wanted more. He said, 'Just a mouthful.' She filled up the cup and handed it back to him. He said, 'You must think I have a big mouth.' She answered, 'I measured by mine.' Grandmother liked him."

Royall House, who was named for him, said that if "Mr. Cooke arrived about 10:30 in the morning, my mother knew that he expected to stay for dinner, so set another place at the table."

Cooke not only was concerned to minister to his congregation but was involved in the life of the area. He was Trustee and Clerk of Brentsville District School Board and a Red Cross Solicitor.

An Aweful Driver

When Cooke first arrived at Greenwich, he drove a buggy. "He had a horse named Maude with whom he was often aggravated," said Raymond Spittle. "He reserved a tree near the gate in front of the church, and here he hitched Maude. He was jealous of his parking space," said Herbert Wood.

Selma Corder remembers that the Ellises furnished Mr. Cooke hay for the horse. One day Johnny Ellis and Selma took hay up to the manse. Cooke was in the garden plowing but joined them. Selma was up in the loft while Johnny Ellis pitched up the hay. All of sudden Johnny yelled at Preacher Cooke to go see about the animal because horse flies were after it. She was kicking and jumping. The preacher dashed there hollering at the top of his voice. "Whoa, Maude-ee Whoa, Maude-ee. Whoa!"

On another occasion, while Cooke was plowing in the garden, he was overheard to say, "Maude you fool, get off the beans!"

The size of the congregation moved quickly from around 60 to 124 by 1911. It soon reached 147. (By 1941 it had dropped to 127.) To reach his various preaching points and pastoral charges, Cooke drove a number of miles and hours. Eventually, the congregation got together and took up a collection. They purchased a car for him. He was better used to directing Maude and the buggy. "He drove awful," said Lucie Reid and several others. One day he came wheeling up to the church and apparently he didn't know how to use the brakes. He drove round and round the lot and finally headed to his favorite parking spot. The car kept going until he hit the tree. "Now," he said slowly; "I'll reckon you'll stop."

Selma Corder worked with the Ellises on the farm and stayed with Johnny Ellis. One day he was way over in the west field plowing, and he heard and saw Mr. Johnny and his wife calling and waving a white cloth for him to come in. Selma unhooked the three horses and went back to the house. He found that Mr. Cooke was there and ready to go home, but his car wouldn't move. It was February and cold. He had come calling at the Ellises and had crossed Broad Run at Raccoon Ford in his Model A Ford. The brakes had gotten wet and later frozen. Selma went into the kitchen and got a tea kettle of boiling water, poured it on the brakes and thawed things out. Cooke remained calm.

One day J. Royall drove the car into Washington, D.C. He didn't motor down Constitution Avenue any better than he did on Vint Hill Road. It wasn't long before the police stopped him. They talked with him a bit but did not arrest or fine him. They decided to get him out of the city as fast as possible "for your sake." A patrol car escorted him to the city limits. A reporter stopped at the incident to see what was going on. The Reverend, his car, several patrol vehicles and policemen on the busy street were caught by a newsphotographer. The next day the picture and the article appeared in the *Washington Post*. The Rev. Mr. Cooke never volunteered information about his escapade, but George M. Wood spotted the item in the paper.

Cooke was hard on automobiles, even after he moved back to Goldvein. Thelma Louise Edwards (Mrs. H. P. Monroe), who grew up there and had been a member of the Grove Presbyterian Church, said that his "auto was all beat up. He drove his old car most anywhere. He'd just travel through the woods and hit two or three trees and keep on going." Cooke liked to hunt and fish, and maybe it made little difference to him whether there was a road or not.

We Toiled All Night

Cooke had learned to fish on the Rappahannock. At Greenwich he often shook out his pole on Broad Run. His favorite hole was near where the present dam for Lake Manassas is situated. "If he took a notion to go fishing, he would go by the House dairy around 7 in the morning and dig worms in the barn while workers were finishing up milking," said Royall House. Sometime he would help with clean up, especially if he wanted company for fishing.

Selma Corder said Mr. Cooke went fishing a lot on the Broad Run with Johnny Ellis who had a bad case of rheumatism. Johnny rode his horse to the creek, and Mr. Cooke walked. They sat there all morning. Sometimes they came back to the house to eat lunch and then went back fishing in the afternoon. They didn't care whether or not they caught anything. Church members often kidded him about, "We toiled all night and took nothing."

He liked to quail hunt as well as go after the rabbits and often took Royall House with him. He was a pretty good shot, but occasionally when the dog pointed and they got into a convey, he found he hadn't even loaded his gun. He also went back to Mt. Ephraim some 30 miles away to hunt. While hunting or fishing, he liked to swap tales. He might talk about Christianity and tell younger companions Bible stories. Donnie Squires owns the 30 U.S. bolt action rifle that Cooke gave Heading Earle Squires.

Cooke was an "old timer who seemed to stay on and on," said James Cooke (no relation). Some may have thought he should have left earlier, but he remained. Eventually, his physical strength waned. At the Session meeting April 9, 1935, he asked for a leave of absence until his health was restored sufficiently to take up his work. He requested leave for one month at the Session meeting July 11, 1936. At the October 11, 1941 meeting, "The Pastor stated that his health was failing and that his throat at times made it very difficult for him to preach." He requested a congregational meeting be called to present his resignation in December.

The pastor smoked a pipe and cigarettes. Prolonged exposure to tobacco caused cancer of the lip. Eventually, surgeons operated. Treatment left him somewhat disfigured and caused him problems keeping liquids in his mouth. When he drank water, he had to hold his lip shut with his finger. He had a problems with saliva.

At his last Session meeting, "The Pastor was requested to turn the key of the Manse over to the President of the Woman's Auxiliary." He preached his final sermon on December 15, 1941 just as the nation geared up for war. He was 71.

"Many loved him like a father," and several still remember him fondly. In the beginning, Cooke had found "his congregation scattered and somewhat divided. He quickly and steadily brought them together again. He laid the foundation with patience and maintained it in the face of many discouragements down across the years."[15]

Cooke returned to Goldvein where he lived with his brother Keith. Like J. R., Keith had no children of his own.[16] Members of the Greenwich congregation occasionally asked J. R. to help with funerals and other pastoral functions. He married sisters, Barbara and Kay Wood, at Mt. Ephraim in a double wedding ceremony in 1943.

One time J. Royall was on the way to Florida to see Nannie Middlethon, and he stopped in Columbus, Georgia. to see his brother, Dr. W. L. Cooke. Selma Corder was in the army and stationed at Ft. Benning, and he went by to see him. Selma said that at that time Preacher Cooke was very feeble.[17]

The former minister last spoke at Greenwich on October 10, 1948 when Reverend Al Winn was installed as pastor. Mae Ellis remembers visiting him at Mt. Ephraim a week before he died of cancer May 16, 1949.

According to his obituary in the Minutes of the Synod of Virginia,

> Cooke...was a man of deep convictions and a sincere lover of the truth. In all these fields of service, his character was what counted most with those who knew him. The best description of that character is that he was a good man, not in the cheap and shallow way in which that word is sometimes used, but in the sense in which it was used of Barnabas. Another life has been completed on this earth of going about and doing good.... "Servant of God, well done."[18]

Cooke had requested that he be buried by his mother. He was laid to rest in the family plot at Grove Presbyterian Cemetery, Goldvein, Virginia.

End Notes

Chapter One - A Distant Drum

1. Donald C. Pfanz, *Richard S. Ewell: A Soldier's Life* (Chapel Hill: The University of North Carolina Press, 1998), pp.2, 263.

2. Samuel J. Martin, *The Road to Glory: Confederate General Richard S. Ewell* (Indianapolis: Guide Press of Indiana, Inc., 1991), p. 215.

3. Pfanz, p. 552, f.n. 30.

4. Michael A. Palmer, *Lee Moves North: Robert E. Lee on the Offensive* (New York: John Wiley & Sons, Inc., 1998), pp. 116, 117.

5. Betty Gray Fitzhugh Snydor, Diary. Original in the possession of Lindsay C. Hope, Purcellville, Virginia.

6. Dudley Fitzhugh lived across the road and Thomas Fitzhugh at Prospect on the present State Highway 603, close to St. Stephen's Church. Thomas apparently went to Tennessee after the war. His wife, Isabella, died at Ringwood in 1876, according to a marker in Greenwich Presbyterian Cemetery.

7. Pfanz, p. 13.

8. Mrs. Jane Gray Davis to Earle P. Barron, November 1998, personal communication.

9. Included in the diary is a map of the area which shows a church on Baldwin Ridge Road. The church building is gone, but an unkept cemetery near it remains just north of the road. Mrs. Jane Gray Davis who currently lives in that area says that it was an Episcopal Church linked with St. James in Warrenton, and the Rev. Otis Barton was the minister in the 1800's. Mrs. Davis attended the Baldwin Ridge Church and the school across the road from it in the 1920's. Dumfries Road went between the two, and the old road bed is still visible. She says Grays and Mitchells were members there at the church, and some were buried in the

cemetery. A stone marker in the graveyard reads, "R. Tasker Mitchell M.D., Feb. 14, 1831, Died About Sept. 1891."

10. *Old Homes and Families of Fauquier County, Virginia* (The W.P.A. Records) (Berryville, Va.: Virginia Book Co., 1978), p. 425.

11. Ibid., pp. 427, 428.

12. Ibid., pp. 429, 430.

13. Eugene M. Scheel, *The Guide to Fauquier: A Survey of The Architecture and History of a Virginia County With 15 Walking Tours of Towns and Villages* (Warrenton, Va.: Warrenton Printing & Publishing, 1976), p. 38. The house is gone but the cemetery remains.

Chapter Two - Rogues Road

1. Carla Johnson, "The War at Table: The South's Struggle for Food," *Columbiad, A Quarterly Review of the War Between the States,* Vol. 1, No. 2, (Summer 1997): pp. 22,23.

2. Lee Maffett, *The Diary of Court House Square: Warrenton, Virginia, USA, From Early Times through 1986 with 1987 - 1995 Reflections,* rev. ed. (Baltimore, Md.: Heritage Books, Inc., 1996), p.36, quoted with permission.

3. Mary Jackson (Jacksie) Howison (1843 - 1872), Diary [photocopy]. The original cannot be located. John Laws, Midland, Virginia, possesses a typewritten copy. Quoted with permission. In the 1860 Census, Jacksie appears to be a member of the family of Stephen Howison, 84, Brentsville farmer. Jane is 55, Samuel 18. Samuel, Co. 6, 49th Va. Inf. was wounded at Gettysburg. Mary J. (Jacksie) 16 and Lucretia 16. [Twins?] Susannah 10. Jacksie married Samuel M. Laws, had 2 children and died at the age of 29 years. David Anderson Turner, *Prince William County (Va.) 1860: An Annotated Census* (Manassas, Va., 1993), p. 70.

4. William A. Brent, Co. A. 7th Virginia Cavalry, C.S.A., *"Memoirs and Recollections of the Civil War"* about 1896 - 1900,

AMs [typed photocopy], p. 31. The original cannot be located. Lawrence D. Brent, Warrenton, Virginia, has a copy. Quoted with his permission.

    5. T. B. Balch, S.T.D., *My Manse During the War: A Decade of Letters to the Rev. J. Thomas Murray, Editor of the Methodist Protestant* (Baltimore: Sherwood & Co., 1866), p.6.

    6. *Old Homes and Families of Fauquier County*, p. 620.

    7. Ibid.

    8. Samuel W. Floca, Jr. and James L. Cooke, "Overdue at Catlett's Station: John S. Mosby's First Yankee Train," *Confederate Veteran*, vol. 3 (1995): pp. 23 - 31.

    9. James Cooke to Earle P. Barron, December 1998, personal communication. There will be no further reference to James Cooke when the text says, "James Cooke said..."

    10. Susan Berkeley Alrich Low, *"The Beautiful and Useful Life of one, of whom His Sons and Daughters may be justly proud, and ever hold in high regard and loving memory, Douglass Moxley Low. His wife, Frances Marion Green, shares this honor with him."* (Composition Book), Archives, Fauquier Historical Society, Warrenton, Virginia, pp. 2-4.

    11. Brent, pp. 29 - 31.

    ˙ 12. Ripley Robinson to Earle P. Barron, December 19, 1998, personal communication.

    13. John Walters, *Norfolk Blues: The Civil War Diary of the Norfolk Light Artillery Blues,* ed. with a forward by Ken Wiley (Shippensburg, Pa.: Burd Street Press, 1997), p. 97.

Chapter Three - A Hamlet On A Hill

    1. Balch, p. 24.

    2. Pfanz, pp. 235, 510, f.n.51. In 1864 Sorrel became a brigadier general. He was wounded in the leg near Petersburg and shot through the lung at Hatcher's Run in 1865 but survived.

    3. Mae Ellis to Earle P. Barron, 1990, personal communication. Wallace Wood took over after Daniel House died

in 1901. It was vacant for a while after Wallace Wood gave it up until Hilary and Carrington Carrico took over. The store burned in 1923.

4. General Beauregard was in charge of the defense of Savannah towards the end of the War. For this he received no glory as he had at Manassas. Instead, he was accused of abandoning Savannah to Sherman. In 1922 Gustave Toutant Beauregard, grandson of P.G.T., married Mildred Furman Green, grandaughter of Charles Green, a possibility that neither P.G.T. nor Charles would have forseen. Mildred Furman Green Beauregard (1901-1935) is buried in the front east section of the Greenwich Presbyterian Church Cemetery. Douglas Green, her father, is also buried in the cemetery. Gustave Toutant Beauregard, Mildred's husband, a lawyer, a captain in the U.S. Army in World War I, is buried in Arlington. Brian Deitch, "Gustave Toutant, Beauregard and the Green Family: In Search of a Namesake of General P.G.T. Beauregard," a research report submitted to Professor Joseph Harsh, George Mason University, in partial fulfillment of requirements for History 390: Battlefields of the Civil War, (August 8, 1986) [photocopy].

5. Balch, p. 24.

6. *War Letters, 1862 - 1865 of John Chipman Gray, Major, Judge Advocate and John Coldman Ropes, Historian of the War, with Portraits* (Boston: Houghton Mifflin Company, The Riverside Press Cambridge, 1927) p. 3.

7. Charles Green Mackall, Jr. to Earle P. Barron, August 21, 1990, transcript in the possession of Earle P. Barron.

8. Ann Green, *With Much Love* (New York: Harper & Brothers Publisher, 1948), p. 5.

9. Julian Green, *Memories of Happy Days* (New York: Harper & Brothers Publishers, 1942), p. 209.

10. Jean Eric Green to Earle P. Barron, February 2, 1992. Transcript in the possession of Earle P. Barron.

11. Ann Green, p. 4.

12. General Mackall was relieved of command at his request after the Battle of Chickamauga. He took command again

under General Joseph E. Johnston January 1864. He requested to be relieved of duty because he didn't want to be under General Hood in front of Atlanta.

13. Elaine Spittle Yankey, "Boley Family Stories." TMs, n.d., original in the possession of Elaine S. yankey, Nokesville, Virginia.

14. Balch, p. 24.

15. John Chipman Gray, p. 166.

16. Low, p. 32.

17. "Moxley Memorial Manse" Scrapbook, Archives Division, Virginia State Library. Richmond, Virginia.

Chapter Four - A Little Brick Church

1. Greenwich Church owns another cemetery. White Hall Presbyterian Church was organized around 1900 near the intersection of Aden Road (State Highway 646) and Brookfield (State Highway 854) close to Nokesville. Some of the members from Greenwich Church helped start it and moved their membership there. It never did too well, and the church was closed. The building was demolished in 1940, perhaps by fire. Some of the members joined Greenwich. The cemetery was in use before the church was organized. At least one victim of the Civil War is buried there. A grave stone indicates that a young soldier from Alabama died of typhoid fever in 1861. There are a number of unlettered stone markers. The cemetery was turned over to Greenwich Church. The cemetery is in poor condition. Some evidence reveals that a Presbyterian Church existed there in the early 1800's. See E.R. Conner, III, *100 Old Cemeteries of Prince William County, Va.* (Manassas, Va.: Lake Lithograph, INC., 1981), pp. 128, 129, 130.

2. Balch, p. 24.

3. Hugh C. Miller, *Notes on Virginia: Virginia Department of Historic Resources,* no. 23 (fall 1989): 14. There is an early picture of the church painted white and one later of it

painted red. The paint has now been removed from the brick. At one time a white board fence enclosed the church yard. In one picture of the fence, two men standing may be Philip M. Boley (1857 - 1929) and Charled Edwin Brady (1845 - 1915). Later, an iron picket fence replaced the board fence. Presently a wooden rail fence borders the front yard. Archives, Greenwich Presbyterian Church.

4. Charles J. Gillis, *A History of the Greenwich Presbyterian Church, Prince William County, Va. 1810 - 1953* and Reba C. Hopkins and Michael E. Giboney, 1953 - 1977.

5. Pfanz, p. 160.

6. Eugene M. Scheel, *The Civil War in Fauquier County Virginia* (Warrenton, Va.: The Fauquier National Bank, 1985), p. 16.

7. *'My Heart Is So Rebellious': The Caldwell Letters 1861 - 1865*, ed. J. Michael Welton, annot. by John K. Gott & John E. Divine, intro. by T. Triplett Russell (Bell Gale Chevigny, n.d.), p. 190 quoted with permission. John W. Pugh was a Lieutenant, Brookes' Artillery C Battery A, 12th Batt'n, Poague's Battalion of Artillery, Jackson's Corps.

8. Helen Jeffries Klitch, ed., *Joseph Arthur Jeffries' Fauquier County, Virginia, 1840 - 1919: Correspondence of Joseph Arthur Jeffries, Fauquier County, Virginia, Confederate Soldier, 1861-1870 and Fauquier County History, Personalities, Anecdotes: The Collected Writings of Joseph A. Jeffries, Warrenton, Virginia, 1840 - 1919* (San Antonio, Tex.: Phil Bate Associate 1989), p.28, quoted with permission.

9. William E. Thompson *"A Set of Rebellious Scoundrels": Three Centuries of Presbyterians along the Potomac* (Hampden-Sydney, Va. William E. Thompson, 1989), p. 76.

10. William D. Henderson, *41st Virginia Infantry* (Lynchburg, Va.: H.E. Howard, Inc., 1986), p. 132.

11. Alexander Hunter, *The Women of the Debatable Land* (Washington, D.C.: Corden Publishing Company, 1912), pp. 215 - 228.

12. J. Richard Winter, *The Story of a Church: A History of the Warrenton Presbyterian Church, Warrenton, Virginia 1771 - 1976*, p. 8.

13. Pfanz, pp. 266, 279.

Chapter Five - Prince William Mud

1. Eugene M. Scheel, *Crossroads and Corners: A Tour of the Villages, Towns and Post Offices of Prince William County, Virginia Past and Present: A Companion Book to the 1992 Historical Map of Prince William County,* ed. Sandra Robinette (Historic Prince William, Inc., 1996), pp. 6,7, quoted with permission.

2. Mae Ellis to Earle P. Barron, 1990, personal communication. Sisters Ella and Annie never married. Hattie married and had two children. Two brothers, Douglas and Keith, married but had no children.

3. Newman Hopkins to Earle P. Barron, 1990, personal communication.

4. Minnie McMichael to Earle P. Barron, December 1998, personal communication.

5. Martin, p. 262.

6. Scheel, *Crossroads and Corners,* pp. 52, 53.

7. Minutes, Greenwich Presbyterian Church Session records other than the original combined Warrenton-Greenwich records before 1894 are lost. This original is at Warrenton Presbyterian Church of Warrenton, Virginia. Minutes from 1894 to the present are at Archives Division, Virginia State Library, Richmond, Virginia. Other material is at the Department of History, (Montreat), Montreat, North Carolina. Microfilm copies of the minutes at Virginia State Library are on file at the Greenwich Church archives.

8. Balch, p. 6.

9. Ibid., p. 40.

10. Ibid., p. 14.

11. Ibid., p. 37.

12. Ibid., pp. 3, 4.

13. Ibid., p. 33.

14. Ibid., p. 14.

15. Thompson, p. 87.

16. Balch, p. 4.

17. Ibid., p. 15.

18. S. Somerville Mackall, *Early Days of Washington* (Washington, D.C.: The Neale Company, 1899), pp. 107, 108.

19. Balch, p. 27.

20. Ibid., p. 38.

21. Ibid., p. 13.

22. Ibid., p. 5.

23. Ibid., p. 39.

24. Ibid., p. 5.

25. Ibid., p. 15.

26. Ibid., p. 12.

27. Pfanz, p. 530, f.n. 20.

28. Ibid., p. 531, f.n. 23.

29. Perry Gatling Hamlin, *"Old Bald Head" (General R.S. Ewell) The Portrait of a Soldier* (Strasburg, Va.: Shenandoah Publishing House, Inc., 1940), p. 4.

30. Pfanz, p. 47.

31. General R.S. Ewell, *The Making of a Soldier: Letters of General R.S. Ewell*, ed. Captain Percy Hamlin, M.D., M.C., Medical Corps National Guard, U.S., Maryland (Richmond, Va.: Whittet & Shepperson, 1935), p. 140.

32. Ibid., p. 110.

33. Balch, p. 40.

34. Pfanz, p. 155.

35. Ibid., pp. 341, 342.

Chapter Six - A Gloomy Scene

1. Colonel Charles S. Wainwright, *A Diary of Battle: The Personal Journals of Colonel Charles S. Wainwright 1861 - 1865*, Allan Nevins, ed. (New York: Da Capo Press, 1998, first published 1962), p. 292.

2. Pfanz, p. 340.

3. William D. Henderson, *The Road to Bristoe Station: Campaigning with Lee and Meade August 1 - October 22, 1863*, The Virginia Civil War Battles and Leaders Series (Lynchburg, Va.: H.E. Howard, Inc., 1987), p. 192.

4. Ibid., p. 194.

5. D'Ann Evans, *Prince William County: A Pictorial History* (Norfolk: The Donning Company Publishers, 1989), p. 59.

6. Rev. Alexender Broadnax Carrington (1833 - 1910) was born in Charlotte County, Virginia and practiced law before becoming a minister. He entered the Confederate Army, 37th Virginia Regt. as a private, but was soon made a chaplain. He took his last pastorate at Greenwich in 1884 and finished his ministry in 1896. He purchased a house and land at 9513 Rogues Road (State Highway 602). Carrington was a frugal man. He fussed about his cook never preparing enough food when at the same time he told her not to fix too much. A neighbor, Tom Kent, let his hogs run out in the commons. An old sow of his got in the Reverend's garden one night and practically ruined it. Carrington penned her up and told Tom that unless he paid him for the garden he would keep the sow. After a while, the sow had a litter of pigs. Tom bided his time. One night when there was no moon, he loaded the old sow and pigs in his light sprint-wagon. By break of day, he was in Stafford County where he sold the lot. Carrington was outdone. James L. Cooke, "A Brief Account of the Life of the Rev. Alexander Broadmax Carrington," 1989, Original in the possession of James L. Cooke, Nokesville, Virginia. The church has books from Carrington's library donated by Mr. Arthur Rudman, Bowie, Maryland.

7. Amanda Virginia Edmonds, *Journals of Amanda Virginia Edmonds, Lass of the Mosby Confederacy 1859 - 1867*,

ed. Nancy Chappalear Baird (Stephens City, Va.: Commercial Press, 1984), quoted with permission.

8. Pfanz, p. 503.

Chapter Seven-The Baroness and Rogues Road

1. Fairfax Harrison, *Landmarks of Old Prince William: A Study in Origins in Northern Virginia*, 2nd reprint edition, vols. 1, 2 (Baltimore: Gateway Press, Inc., 1987), vol. 2, for Prince William Historic Commission, pp. 443-445.

2. Kay Wood Beach to Earle P. Barron, 1990, personal communication.

3. Harrison, p. 460.

4. Baroness Fredericke Reidisel, *Letters and Journals: Eye Witness Accounts of the American Revolution* (New York: The New York Times & Arno Press, n.d.), p. 159.

Chapter Eight - The Peculiar Institution

1. Evans, p. 89.

2. *Letters and Family Documents Relating to Charles Green of Savannah, Georgia and Greenwich, Virginia* (Privately printed by General Offset Company, Inc. 1941).

3. Nancy Alderman, "A Biography of Charles Green" (Manuscript for Dr. Roger Warlick, 1980), [Photocopy] Archives, Historical Society, Savannah, Georgia.) p.7.

4. Ann Green, pp. 1,3.

5. Klitch, p. 1.

6. Ann Green, p. 1.

7. Minnie McMichael to Earle P. Barron, December 1990, personal communication.

8. Ann Green, p. 1.

9. Minutes, Session, Warrenton and Greenwich Presbyterian Churches, 1855 - 1867, June 10, 1860.

10. Ibid.

11. Robert Bell Woodsworth, *A History of the Presbytery of Winchester: Its Rise and Growth, Ecclesiastical Relations, Churches and Ministers Based on Official Documents* (Staunton, Va.: The McClure Printing Co., 1947), p. 448.

12. *Savannah Newspaper Digest*, Jan. 1 - Dec. 31, 1853, p. 231.

13. Ann Green, p. 3.

14. Mr. & Mrs. Harmon House, "The House Family From Diersheim, Germany in 1817: With Supplement of Henry House, Morgan County, Indiana" [Photocopy] Archives, Greenwich Presbyterian Church, Nokesville, Virginia.

15. Richard E. Beringer, Herman, Hattaway, Archer Jones, and William N. Still, Jr., *Why the South Lost the Civil War* (Athens: The University of Georgia Press, 1986), p. 417.

16. Robert Turner to Earle P. Barron, December 1990, personal communication, December 1998.

17. Ripley Robinson to Earle P. Barron, personal communication.

18. "Letters and Family Documents Relating To Charles Green..."

Chapter Nine-An Eccentric Clergyman

1. Thomas Willing Balch, A.B, "Notices of Six Presbyterian Divines Bearing the Name of Balch," *Journal of the Presbyterian Historical Society* 3, no. 2 (June 1905): 79 - 85.

2. S. Somervell Mackall, *Early Days of Washington* (Washington: The Neale Company, 1899), pp. 107,108.

3. Thomas Willing Balch, p. 85.

4. Thomas Bloomer Balch, "Summer in the Blue Ridge," *Southern Literary Messenger* 15 (1849): 80.

5. Woodsworth, p. 148.

6. See page 87. number 4.

7. Donald L. Wilson, "Title Search" [Property of Thomas B. Balch] TD [Photocopy], July 31, 1981.

8. E. P. Miller, *Ringwood Manse a Pastoral Poem* (Washington, D.C.: "School of Music" Print, 1887), p. 20.

9. Mackall, p. 108.

10. Klitch, pp. 143, 144.

11. Miller, pp. 21, 22.

12. Klitch, p. 144.

13. Minutes, Potomac Presbytery, September 12, 1861, p. 7.

14. Minutes, Rappahannock Presbytery, October 5, 1866; June 1867; October 18, 1867, pp. 26, 413, 65, 46.

15. "Letters and Family Documents Relating to Charles Green..."

16. W.W. Corcoran, *A Grandfather's Legacy: Containing A Sketch of His Life and Obituary Notices of Some Members of His Family Together With Letters from His Friends* (Washington: Henry Polkenhorn, Printer, 1879), p. 310.

17. Minutes, Chesapeake Presbytery, April 1878, p. 155.

18. Thompson, p. 43.

19. Thomas Willing Balch, *Balch Genealogical* (Philadelphia: Allen, Lane and Scott, 1907) pp. 372, 373. Also, Galusha Burchard Balch, *Geneology of the Balch Families* (Salem, Mass.: Putnam, 1897). pp. 459,475.

20. Klitch, p. 144.

21. David Anderson Turner, *Prince William County (Va.) 1860: An Annotated Census* (Manassas, Va., 1993), pp. 6,7. Mary L. and Julia Balch were classified as students. There were 9 slaves. In the 1870 census, John H. Carter, 72, apparently a relative of Susan's, along with Julia R. Chaliners and William Chalmers, lived at home. In addition, Sallie Brown, 70, a free black, and Rebecca Dolson, 25, servant, and her two children lived there. Ronald Ray Turner, *Prince William County (Va.) 1870: Annotated Census* (Manassas, Va., 1993), pp. 6,7.

22. Minutes and Register, Session, Warrenton and Greenwich Presbyterian Churches, 1855-67.

23. Thomas Willing Balch, *Balch Genealogical,* pp. 363,364.

Chapter Ten-A Man Of Means

1. "Mr. Green and General Sherman," *Savannah Morning News*, December 20, 1964.

2. Low, p. 32.

3. Nancy Alderman, p. 9.

4. Burke Davis, *Sherman's March* (New York: Random House, 1980) p. 123.

Chapter Eleven-The Beloved Teacher

1. Agnes Wood Godfrey to Earle P. Barron, 1990, personal communication.

2. E. P. Miller, pp. 53,54.

3. *Old Homes and Families of Fauquier County*, p. 620.

4. "Local Family Charts 300 years of Freedom," *Journal Messenger*, February 12, 1990. Also, Elizabeth Nickens to Earle P. Barron, February 1990, personal communication.

5. Plot 65. The same monument has an inscription to John Story Gulick (1816-1884) Pay Director U. S. Navy and his wife Elizabeth Milligan (1813-1893). Elizabeth Gulick is recorded in the Warrenton-Greenwich Session Minutes (1855-1867), p. 24, as having "Been ordered to be dropped from the roll, by reason of having removed to a distance permanently, without having applied for dismission without a reasonable time." Janie Milligan is listed in the same minutes, register D. The cemetery plot includes what appear to be other members of the family who were moved from Holmead Cemetery. Jeffries said the Misses Milligan "removed their Seminary for young ladies from Rock Hill to Culpeper." Klitch, p. 55.

Chapter Twelve-The Wicked Storekeeper

1. Minutes, Session, Warrenton-Greenwich Presbyterian Churches (1855 - 1867) pp. 3, 11, 12, 24. The joint Session met when business needed to be conducted at whichever church the business related to.

2. The 1850 Census book shows "John Kulp - 57 farmer, wife - Catherine - 55, and children Elizabeth 22, Aron 20, Amelia 16." The Deed Book of Prince William County shows a transaction from "Henry Barron to John Kulp of Montgomery County, Penn. 64 acres." (known later as Veeder Farm) (Deed Book #16, Prince William County (Va.), 1839, p. 77.) Kulp sold to Charles Green, 10 December 1856. Another transaction shows "John Kulp and Catherine, his wife, to James H. Moore - 1 1/4 acres where the said Moore now lives including the blacksmith shop. 'Can use the well on adjoining lot for all uses.'" (Deed Book #23, Prince William County (Va.), Aug. 12, 1853, p. 195.) Did John Kulp own/operate the store on the corner of State Highway 215 and State Highway 603 which was located in what is now the parking lot of Mayhugh's Store?

Chapter Thirteen-The Poor Preacher

1. Minutes, Chesapeake Presbytery, November 9, 10, 22, 1877.

2. Ripley Robinson to Earle P. Barron, December 19, 1998, personal communication.

3. Minutes, Synod of Virginia, October 1893, p. 342.

Chapter Fourteen-An Old Timer

1. Jane was 24 years younger than John. The Chief Justice expressed his concern about Jane's romance with Major George

Keith Taylor in a letter to his brother, James M. Marshall. He believed that George was not suitable for Jane even though a gentleman of talents and integrity. He felt he possessed little fortune, was encumbered with a family and did not like his profession. John Marshall thought Jane had concealed the "lover" relationship from him and that Jane had revealed too much "partiality for him." "This affair embarrasses me a good deal," he said. Jane married George Keith Taylor within a few months. Taylor proved to be a man of unusual ability and high character, and he became very successful in his profession. President Adams appointed him U. S. Judge for Virginia district in 1801. It was a happy union. A large portrait of Jane hung at Mt. Ephraim until 1951. Albert J. Beveridge, *The Life of John Marshall: Politician, Diplomatist, Statesman 1789-1801* 4 vols. (Boston: Houghton Mifflin Company, 1916), 2:174, 175. They lived at Spring Garden near Petersburg, Virginia. Judge Taylor died in 1815. For a while Jane ran a girl's school in the city, and then she returned to Mt. Ephraim. Frances Norton Mason, *My Dearest Polly: Letters of Chief Justice John Marshall to His Wife, with Their Background, Political and Domestic, 1779-1831* (Richmond, Va.: Garrett & Massie, 1961), p. 351.

2. *Old Homes and Families* pp. 738, 739. *Christian Observer* (Philadelphia), February 28, 1856.

3. Fauquier County Bicentennial Committee, *Fauquier County, Virginia 1759 - 1959.* (Warrenton, Va.: Virginia Publishing, Inc., 1959), pp. 198, 199. The women present were likely Jane Marshall Taylor who died there in 1866, her daughter Anna Keith Royall and Anna's daughter, Helen Matilda Cooke, who died there in 1900. The house site may be reached by taking State Highway 641 west off of 17 and then making a left onto State Highway 615, continuing on State Highway 803 until public maintenance runs out. A dirt road to the right leads to the foundation stones about a quarter of a mile away.

4. Another daughter, Mary A., married The Reverend R. L. McMurran. Woodsworth, p. 495.

5. Thomas Jefferson discovered a gold nugget by the Rappahannock River in 1782. By the late 1840's, Virginia was the leading U. S. gold producer. Sporadic mining continued between 1919 - 1938, and the last gold commercially mined in Fauquier County was in 1964, Several mines around Goldvein led to the changing of the name of the community from Grove to Goldvein. Johnson, Liberty and Union Mines were fairly close to Mt. Ephraim. Two large "hornet balls" of reinforced concrete which were used to separate the ore may be seen by the side of the State Highway 651, .8 of a mile west of highway 17 at the Liberty Mine site. Eugene M. Scheel, *The Guide to Fauquier: A Survey of the Architecture and History of a Virginia County* (Warrenton, Va.: Warrenton Printing and Publishing, 1976), p. 44.

6. The canal was begun by 1829 to get around the rapids in the river between Fredericksburg and Waterloo. There were 44 locks and 20 dams. Most of the locks were of granite stones. The dams were of rock extending across the river. The venture was not profitable, and railroads put an end it its use by 1868. The walls of Lock #14, just below Mt. Ephraim, are in good condition. Remains of Skinker's Mill are nearby the lock. Fauquier County Bicentennial Committee, *Fauquier County, Virginia 1759-1959* (Warrenton, Va.), pp 109-113.

7. Minutes, General Assembly, Presbyterian Church, U. S., 1972, part II, p. 158. Mrs. N. K. Middelthon, historian, "History of Grove Church, 1943, Potomac Presbytery, Goldvein, Virginia." The white frame building was then sold and moved about 3/4 mile down State Highway 615 and then State Highway 617 to where it stands in a pine field. The new owner elevated the church, added a first floor beneath and tried to convert the structure into an apartment building. He never completed the project. Grove Baptist Church, at the site of the village of Grove or Goldvein, had 120 resident members in 1989. The Baptist reluctantly inherited the Grove Presbyterian Cemetery which is across the road from the Baptist burial place. They reserve it for non member burials. Doretta French, "History of Grove Baptist Church," TMs [mimeographed], 1989. An immense oak tree inside the gate of the

Grove Baptist Church was cause to remember William L. Royall, a scout for the Confederates who was captured by Federals and sentenced to be hung as a spy. The rope was in place, and he was asked if he had anything to say. He spoke so eloquently that he brought tears to the Union officer who said it would be a shame to kill such a bright young man. His life was spared, and afterwards he became a lawyer and was largely responsible for settling the debt question with West Virginia. *Old Homes and Families of Fauquier County, Virginia,* pp. 103-105. Doretta French said that Royall or a man by the name of Royall was caught and "managed to convince them that he was a 'Union Man' and they let him go. He was, in truth, a spy for both sides." The Yankees left only walls and roof to the building. Around 1912, "The Manse" property for the Presbyterian Church which belonged to Rev. J. J. Royall was sold to W. L. Royall, grandson of J. J., perhaps the same person as above. He changed the name of the site to "Locust Hill." *Old Homes and Families of Fauquier County Virginia,* p. 739. John Royall Cooke's brother, W. L., may have been named for him.

8. Cooke probably went to school at Pine View, Va. which was between Goldvein and Summerduck. The school house was at the intersection of State Highways 651 and 631 (Royall's Road). The school house was torn down, and the old store across the road moved to that site where it stands presently on the corner. Pine View Post Office where the Cookes received their mail was closed around 1940. Olive V. Jones, *The Little Village of Summerduck (Fifty years ago) Written in 1970* (copyright James J. Durnan, Jr., 1970), pp. 26, 27.

9. During the Civil War, the Presbyterian Church of Kentucky divided into Northern and Southern branches with both claiming control over Centre College. The North won at court and pro Southern persons formed Central University which opened in 1874. The college had financial problems from the outset and never had a graduating class of more than 25. It merged with Centre College in 1901. Property of Central University, as well as old records, eventually were received into what is now Eastern Kentucky University. Charles C. Hay III and Charles D. Whitlock,

"Eastern Kentucky University: A Historical Perspective." TMs [Photocopy] Archives, Greenwich Presbyterian Church, Nokesville, Va., Cooke's courses from "Catalogue of Students," p. 26. Dr. Rutherford E. Douglas, a member of Cooke's class, said that Cooke and two others "had as college students found each a secure place in the esteem of his fellow students and Richmond citizens." Robert Stuart Sanders, *The History of Louisville Presbyterian Theological Seminary* (Louisville: Louisville Seminary, 1953) pp. 28, 29.

10. Cooke ministered at Burnside and Pisgah Churches and was stated supply of Kings Mountain and Pulaski Churches in Transylvania Presbytery from 1894-1898. In 1898 ill health overtook him, and he returned to a farm in Fauquier County, presumably Mt. Ephraim. He served as an occasional stated supply of churches from 1898-1907. Minutes of the Synod of Virginia, Sept. 7-9, 1948, p. 513.

11. Personal communications from church members to Earle P. Barron, December 1991, will be noted in the text.

12. Mrs. Middelthon supported the Young People and they appreciated it. In the late 30's, she planned a trip to Norway to visit her husband's family. The Youth gave her a personalized piece of luggage.

13. A tombstone in Grove Presbyterian Cemetery reads "Gustav Middlethon / July 25, 1867 / May 20, 1920 / Nanie Keith Middelthon / December 9, 1867-December 19, 1963." The name Keith seems to come from the mother of Jane and John Marshall, Mary Randolph Keith, daughter of a minister of the Church of England. Leonard Baker, *John Marshall: A Life in Law* (New York: MacMillan Publishing Co., Inc., 1974), p. 6. The parents of J. Royall also gave another son, G. Keith Cooke, the name. Keith was 13 years younger than J. Royall and died November 1, 1950.

14. "Mr. Cooke had married my brother Wallace and Virginia Bell at the manse in 1934. But he didn't give the fee envelope back to my sister-in-law Virginia Bell. It contained a $10 gold piece that my mother's Aunt Minerva Ross, who had taught

at Ringwood School, had given to Abi Rosso Wood, my mother, to give the minister when the first son was married."

15. Gillis, p. 9.

16. Mr. Hugh Monroe remembered that as a child Keith had told her mother to give her to him so she could sit on his lap, since he had no children to do so.

17. While at Ft. Benning, Selma went to the Presbyterian Church in Columbus, Georgia. One of the hostesses found out he was from Greenwich and asked him if he knew Dr. W. L. Cooke who was then retired. He was introduced, and the Cookes entertained him a number of times on Sunday for dinner and sight seeing. Dr. Cooke had no children.

18. Minutes, Synod of Virginia, September 7-9, 1948, p. 10.

Bibliography

Alderman, Nancy. "A Biography of Charles Green." Manuscript for Dr. Roger Warlick. TMs [photocopy], Archives, Historical Society, Savannah, Ga.

Baird, Nany Chappelear. *Fauquier County, Virginia Tombstone Inscriptions*, n.p., 1970.

_____. *Journals of Amanda Virginia Edmonds: Lass of the Mosby Confederacy 1859 - 1867*. Stephens City, Va. 22655: Commercial Press, 1984.

Baker, Leonard. *John Marshall: A Life in Law*. New York: Macmillan Publishing Co., Inc., 1974.

Balch, Galusha Burchard. *Genealogy of the Balch Families in America*. Salem, Mass.: E. Putnam, 1897.

Balch, Rev. T. B. *Reminiscences of Georgetown, D.C.: A Lecture Delivered in the Methodist Protestant Church, Georgetown, D.C., January 20, 1859*. Washington: Henry Palkinhorn, 1859.

_____. T. B., S.T.D. *My Manse During the War: A Decade of Letters to The Rev. J. Thomas Murray, Editor of the Methodist Protestant*. Baltimore: Sherwood & Co., 1866.

_____. 1793 - 1878. *The Ringwood Discourses*. Hagerstown, Md.: McKee, 1850.

_____. "Summer in the Blue Ridge." *Southern Literary Messenger* 15 (1849): 80.

Balch, Thomas Willing. *Balch Genealogica*. Philadelphia: Allen, Lane and Scott, 1907.

_____. A.B. "Notices of Six Presbyterian Divines Bearing the Name of Balch." *Journal of the Presbyterian Historical Society* 3 (June 1905): 79-85.

Barron, Bob A. *Gold Mines of Fauquier County, Virginia*. Warrenton, Va.: Warrenton Printing & Publishing Co., 1977.

Barron, Henry, deed of sale to John Kulp, 1839, Prince William County, Va. Deed Book 16, p. 77. Microfilm, Reel 12 of Prince William County Records.

Beringer, Richard E., Herman Hattaway, Archer Jones and William N. Still, Jr. *Why the South Lost the Civil War.* Athens: The Unversity of Georgia Press, 1986.

Beveridge, Albert J. *The Life of John Marshall,* vol. 2. *Politician, Diplomat, Statesman 1789 - 1801.* Boston: Houghton Mifflin Company, 1916.

Brent, William A., Co. A. 7th Virginia Cavalry, C.S.A. "Memoirs and Recollections of the Civil Way" about 1896-1900. TMs [photocopy] The original cannot be located. Lawrence D. Brent, Warrenton, Virginia. Has a copy.

Callahan, Donald S. "The Rappahannock Canal, 1972." TMs [photocopy]. Fauquier County Library, Warrenton, Virginia. *Central Presbyterian.* (Richmond), 23 November 1865. *Christian Observer.* (Philadelphia). 28 February 1856.

Conner, E.R., III, *100 Old Cemetaries of Prince William County, Va.* Manassas, Va.: Lake Lithograph, Inc. 1981.

Cooke, James L. "A Brief Account of the Life of The Rev. Alexander Broadnax Carrington, 1989." TMs [photocopy], Archives, Greenwich Presbyterian Church, Nokesville, Virginia.

Corcoran, W.W. *A Granfather's Legacy: Containing a Sketch of His Life and Obituary Notices of Some Members of His Family, Together with Letters From His Friends.* Washington: Henry Polkinhorn, Printer, 1879.

Davis, Burke. *Sherman's March.* New York: Random House, 1980.

Deitch, Brian. "Gustave Toutant Beauregard and the Green Family: In Search of a Namesake of General P.W.T. Beauregard." A Research Report Submitted to Professor Joseph Marsh, George Mason University, 1986. TMs [Photocopy], Archives, Greenwich Presbyterian Church, Nokesville, Virginia.

Fauquier County Bicentennial Committee. *Fauquier County, Virginia 1759 - 1959.* Warrenton Va.: Virginia Publishing, Inc., 1959.

Floca, Samuel W., Jr. and James L. Cooke. "Overdue at Catlett's Station: John S. Mosby's First Yankee Train," *Confederate Veteran,* Vol. 3, 1995.

French, Doretta. "History of Grove Baptist Church, 1986, rev. 1989." TMs [photocopy], Office, Grove Baptist Church, Goldvein, Va.

Gillis, Charles J. *A History of the Greenwich Presbyterian Church, Prince William County, Va., 1810 - 1953* and Hopkins, Reba C. and Giboney, Michael E., *1953 - 1977.*

Gray, John Chipman, and John Codman Ropes. *War Letters 1862 - 1865: With Portraits.* Boston: Houghton Mifflin Company, 1927.

Green, Jean Eric to Earle P. Barron, February 2, 1992, transcript in the possession of Earle P. Barron, Nokesville, Virginia.

Gulick, John S. to The Board of Managers of Oak Hill Cemetery, Georgetown, D.C., April 28, 1874, March 9, 1883, May 14, 1883. ALS, [photocopy] Transcript in the possession of The Board of Managers, Oak Hill Cemetery, Georgetown, D.C.

Hamlin, Captain Percy Gatling, MD, M.C., ed., *The Making of a Soldier: Letters of General R.S. Ewell.* Richmond, Va.: Whittet & Shepperson, 1935.

_____. *"Old Bald Head" (General R.S. Ewell): The Portrait of a Soldier.* Strasburg, Virginia: Shenandoah Publishing House, Inc., 1940.

Harrison, Fairfax. *Landmarks of Old Prince William: A Study in Origins in Northern Virginia,* 2nd reprint ed., vols. 1 and 2. Baltimore: Gateway Press, Inc., 1987 for Prince William County Historical Commission.

Hay, Charles to Earle P. Barron, December 12, 1991. Transcript in the possession of Earle P. Barron, Nokesville, Virginia.

Hay, Charles C., III, and Charles D. Whitlock. "Eastern Kentucky University: A Historical Perspective." TMs [photocopy].

University Archives, Eastern Kentucky University, Richmond, Ky. n.d.

Henderson, William D. *41st Virginia Infantry*. Lynchburg, Va.: H.E. Howard, Inc., 1986.

_____. *The Road to Bristoe: Campaigning with Lee and Meade, August 1 - October 20, 1863*. The Virginia Civil War Battles and Leaders Series. n.p., 1987.

"Honor Roll for 1889 - 90," "Class Lists 1890 - 91. Central University." [photocopy], University Archives, Eastern Kentucky University, Richmond, Kentucky.

Howison, Mary Jackson (Jacksie). Diary. TMs [photocopy]. The original cannot be located. John Laws, Midland, Virginia. Has a copy.

House, Harmon, Mr. and Mrs., "The House Family from Diersheim, Germany in 1817: With Supplement of Henry House, Morgan County, Indiana." TMs [photocopy], Archives, Greenwich Presbyterian Church, Nokesville, Virginia.

Hunter, Alexander. *The Women of the Debatable Land*. Washington, D.C.: Corden Publishing Company, 1912.

Jackson, Mary Francis (Jackie) (1843 - 1872). Diary. TMs [photocopy] in the possession of Earle Barron. Original cannot be located.

Johnson, Carla. "The War at the Table: The South's Struggle for Food." *Columbiad: A Quarterly Review of the War Between the States*, vol. 1 (Summer 1997).

Jones, Olive V. *The Little Village of Sumerduck (Fifty years ago)*. n.p., 1970.

Jones, Virgil Carrington. *Ranger Mosby*. Chapel Hill, N.C.: University of North Carolina Press, 1944.

Kulp, John, deed of sale to James H. Moore, August 12, 1853, Prince William County, Va. Deed Book 23, p. 195. Microfilm, Reel 14 of Prince William County Records.

Low, Susan Berkeley Alrich. "The Beautiful and Useful Life of One, of Whom His Sons and Daughters May Be Justly Proud, and Even Hold in High Regard and Loving

Memory, Douglass Moxley Low, His Wife, Frances Marion Green, Shares This Honor With Him." Composition Book, Archives, Fauquier Historical Society, Warrenton, Virginia.

Mackall, Charles Green, Jr. to Earle P. Barron, August 21, 1990. Transcript in the possession of Earle P. Barron.

Mackall, S. Somervell. *Early Days of Washington.* Washington: The Neale Company, 1899.

Mason, Frances Norton. *My Dearest Polly: Letters of Chief Justice John Marshall to His Wife, with Background, Political and Domestic, 1779 - 1831.* Richmond: Garrett & Massie, 1961.

Middelthon, Mrs. N.K., Historian. "History of Grove Church, Women of the Church, Potomac Presbytery 1943," TMs [photocopy] Archives, Department of History (Montreat), Montreat, N.C.

Miller, E.P. *Ringwood Manse: Pastoral Poem.* Washington, D.C.: "School of Music" print, 1887.

Miller, Hugh C. "The Virginia Landmarks Register." *Notes on Virginia* 33 (Fall 1989), 4 - 17.

Minutes, Chesapeake Presbytery, April 1878, November 9, 10, 22, 1877. ADS, Archives, Department of History (Montreat), Montreat, North Carolina.

Minutes, GA, PCUS, 1972, Part 2. ADS, Archives, Department of History, (Montreat), Montreat, North Carolina.

Minutes, Potomac Presbytery, September 12, 1861. ADS, Archives, Department of History (Montreat), Montreat, North Carolina.

Minutes, Rappahannock Presbytery October 5, 1866; June 1867; October 18, 1867. ADS, Archives, Department of History (Montreat), Montreat, North Carolina.

Minutes, Session, Greenwich Presbyterian Church 1894 - 1920, 1920 - 1940, 1940 - 1949, ADS Archives Division, Virginia State Library, Richmond, Virginia.

Minutes, Session, Warrenton and Greenwich Presbyterian Chuirches 1855 - 1867, TMs from ADS [photocopy],

Archives, Greenwich Presbyterian Church, Nokesville, Virginia.

Minutes, Synod of Virginia, October 1893, September 7 - 9, 1948. ADS, Archives, Department of History (Montreat), Montreat, North Carolina.

Moffett, Lee. *The Diary of Court House Square: Warrenton, Virginia, USA, From Early Times Through 1986, with 1987 - 1995 Reflections. rev. ed.*. Heritage Books, Inc., 1996.

Morning News (Savannah). 20 December 1964.

"Moxley Memorial Manse." Scrapbook. Archives Division, Virginia State Library, Richmond, Virginia.

Nevins, Allan, ed., new foreword, Stephen W. Sears, maps by Rafael Palacios. *A Diary of Battle: The Personal Journals of Colonel Charles S. Wainwright 1861 - 1865.* New York: DaCapo Press, 1998.

Old Homes and Families of Fauquier County, Virginia: W.P.A. Records. Berryville, Va.: Virginia Book Company, 1978.

Palmer, Michael A. *Lee Moves North: Robert E. Lee on the Offensive.* New York: John Wiley & Sons, Inc., 1998.

Pfanz, Donald C. *Richard S. Ewell: A Soldier's Life.* Chapel Hill: The University of North Carolina Press, 1998.

Ramey, Emily G. and John K. Gott, co-chairmen; Gestrude Trumbo and John Eisenhard of *The Fauguier Democrat*, eds. *The Years of Anguish: Fauquier County, Virginia 1861 - 1865.* Berryville, Va.: Virginia Book Company, n.d.

Reidisel, Baroness Fredericke. *Letters and Journals: Eyewitness Accounts of the American Revolution.* New York: The New York Times & Arno Press, n.d.

Sanders, Robert Stuart. *The History of Louisville Presbyterian Theological Seminary.* Louisville: Louisville Seminary, 1953.

Savannah Newspaper Digest (Savannah). 1 January - 31 December 1853.

Scheel, Eugene M. *The Civil War in Fauquier County Virginia.* Warrenton: The Fauquier National Bank, 1985.

_____. Sandra Robinette, ed. *Crossroads and Corners: A Guided Tour of The Villages, Towns and Post Offices of Prince William County, Virginia Past & Present The Companion Book To The 1992 Historical Map of Prince William County.* Prince William, Va.: Historic Prince William, Inc. And Eugene M. Scheel. 1992

_____. *The Guide To Fauquier: A Survey of The Architecture and History of a Virginia County With 15 Walking Tours of Towns and Villages.* Warrenton, Va.: Warrenton Printing & Publishing, 1976.

Siepel, Kevin H. *Rebel: The Life and Times of John Singleton Mosby.* New York: Da Capo Press, 1997.

Snydor, Betty Gray Fitzhugh. Diary. AMs original in the possession of Lindsay G. Hope, Purceliville, Virginia.

Thompson, William E. *A Set of Rebellious Scoundrels: Three Centuries of Presbyterians along the Potomac.* Hampton-Sydney, Va., n.p. September 1989.

Turner, David Anderson. *Prince William County (Va.) 1860: An Annotated Census* Manassas, Va., 1993.

Turner, Ronald Ray, *Prince William County (Va.) 1870: An Annotated Census* Manassas, Va., 1993.

Walters, John. Kenneth Wiley, ed. and introd. *Norfolk Blues: The Civil War Diaries of the Norfolk Light Artillery Blues.* Shippensburg, Pa.: Burd Street Press, 1997.

Welton, J. Michael, ed., John K. Gott & John E. Divine, annots, T. Triplett Russell, introd. *My Heart Is So Rebellious: The Caldwell Letters 1861 - 1865.* Bell Gale Chevigny, n.d.

Wilson, Donald L., "Title Search of property of Thomas Bloomer Balch, Prince William County, Va., July 31, 1981" to James Cooke. TMs [photocopy], Archives, Greenwich Presbyterian Church, Nokesville, Virginia.

Winter, J. Richard. *The Story of a Church: A History of the Warrenton Presbyterian Church Warrenton, Va.* n.p., n.d.

Woodworth, Robert Bell. *A History of the Presbytery of Winchester (Synod of Virginia): Its Rise and Growth, Ecclesiastical Relations, Institutions and Agencies, Churches and Ministers Based on Official Documents.* Staunton, Va., 1947.

Workers of the Writers Program of the W.P.A. in Virginia. *Prince William: The Story of Its People and Its Places.* American Guide Series, Manassas, Va.: Bethlehem Good Housekeeping Club, 1988.

Yankey, Elaine Spittle. "Boley Family Sotries." TMs, n.d. original in the possession of Elaine Spittle Yankey, Nokesville, Virginia.